Corporate Acquisitions and Mergers in Portugal

Corporate Acquisitions and Mergers in Portugal

Second Edition

Marisa Larguinho
Inês Magalhães Correia
Nuno Sobreira

This book was originally published as a chapter in Corporate Acquisitions and Mergers.

General Editor: Peter Begg

Wolters Kluwer

Published by:
Kluwer Law International B.V.
PO Box 316
2400 AH Alphen aan den Rijn
The Netherlands
E-mail: lrs-sales@wolterskluwer.com
Website: www.wolterskluwer.com/en/solutions/kluwerlawinternational

Sold and distributed by:
Wolters Kluwer Legal & Regulatory U.S.
920 Links Avenue
Landisville, PA 17538
United States of America
E-mail: customer.service@wolterskluwer.com

ISBN 978-94-035-3446-6

e-Book: ISBN 978-94-035-3846-4
web-PDF: ISBN 978-94-035-3856-3

Contents

MORAIS LEITÃO, GALVÃO TELES, SOARES DA SILVA & ASSOCIADOS – SOCIEDADE DE ADVOGADOS, SP, RL

Morais Leitão is a leading full-service law firm in Portugal with a solid background of more than eighty years of experience.

Internationally recognised, its reputation stems from the excellence and high level of the services provided to clients, solid ethical values and a distinctive approach with cutting-edge solutions.

Specialised legal services in the main areas of law and in different sectors of the economy are a benchmark of the firm leading to its involvement in the most important operations in Portugal, as well as in high-value cross-border transactions and disputes.

With a team consisting of more than two-hundred lawyers, Morais Leitão has its head office in Lisbon and offices in Porto and Funchal (Madeira Island). To support clients' international strategies, Morais Leitão developed a network of associations with local firms in Angola, Mozambique and Cape Verde – Morais Leitão Legal Circle, which offers integrated multijurisdictional teams.

Firm name: Morais Leitão, Galvão Teles, Soares da Silva & Associados – Sociedade de Advogados, SP, RL [Morais Leitão]

Address: Rua Castilho, 165, 1070-050 Lisboa, Portugal

Tel.: +351 21 381 74 00

Fax: +351 21 381 74 99

Website: www.mlgts.pt

Authors

Marisa Larguinho joined Morais Leitão in September 2019. She is a member of the firm's corporate and M&A and capital markets team.

Her practice focuses on capital markets, M&A, corporate and finance law. She is vastly experienced in assisting in the issuance and offering of capital and debt financial instruments, banking finance transactions and mergers and acquisitions, both at the national and international levels.

Throughout her career, she has regularly advised on transactional and current corporate assistance, listed companies and large company groups in several economic sectors such as banks, energy and communications.

E-mail: mlarguinho@mlgts.pt

Inês Magalhães Correia joined the firm in March 2015. She is a member of the corporate and M&A and capital markets team. She was also part of the litigation and arbitration team.

Inês provides regular legal advice to national and international clients, mainly in the areas of commercial and corporate law, corporate governance and securities law and specifically focuses on M&A transactions, often cross-border, such as share deals, asset deals, partnerships, restructurings, and sales of non-performing loans and distressed assets.

In the field of securities law and capital markets, Inês regularly assists in transactions regarding the issue and offering of equity and debt securities, including medium-term notes and covered bonds.

E-mail: imcorreia@mlgts.pt

Nuno Sobreira joined the firm in September 2013.

He is part of the corporate and M&A and capital markets team, as well as of the cross-practice teams responsible for insurance, reinsurance and pension funds and restructuring and insolvency.

The core of Nuno Sobreira's activity consists of providing legal advisory to national and international clients in M&A transactions, notably sale of shareholdings, partnerships, restructuring processes and asset disposals, including in the banking and insurance sectors. He also has experience in Corporate Governance and financial regulatory compliance matters.

Nuno Sobreira provides regular assistance to listed companies and corporate groups of significant dimensions, mainly in the banking and insurance sectors, in matters of corporate and commercial law.

E-mail: nasobreira@mlgts.pt

Other contributors:

Filipe Vaz Pinto (Litigation and Arbitration)

(https://www.mlgts.pt/en/people/partners/Filipe-Vaz-Pinto/132/)

António Pedro Braga (Tax)

(https://www.mlgts.pt/en/people/partners/Antonio-Pedro-Braga/289/)

Luís do Nascimento Ferreira (European Law and Competition)

(https://www.mlgts.pt/en/people/partners/Luis-do-Nascimento-Ferreira/176/)

Rita Ferreira Vicente (Real Estate)

(https://www.mlgts.pt/en/people/partners/Rita-Ferreira-Vicente/202/)

António Sampaio Caramelo (Litigation and Arbitration)

(https://www.mlgts.pt/en/people/of-counsel/Antonio-Sampaio-Caramelo/44/)

Maria Soares do Lago (Banking)

(https://www.mlgts.pt/en/people/managing-associates/Maria-Soares-do-Lago/45/)

Rui Ribeiro Lima (Public Law)

(https://www.mlgts.pt/en/people/managing-associates/Rui-Ribeiro-Lima/253/)

Paula Ribeiro Farinha (Employment)

(https://www.mlgts.pt/en/people/managing-associates/Paula-Ribeiro-Farinha/237/)

Mariana Soares David (Distribution Agreements)
(https://www.mlgts.pt/en/people/managing-associates/Mariana-Soares-David/245/)
Duarte Santana Lopes (Criminal)
(https://www.mlgts.pt/en/people/managing-associates/Duarte-Santana-Lopes/288/)
Vasco Stilwell d'Andrade (IP)
https://www.mlgts.pt/en/people/partners/Vasco-Stilwell-dAndrade/299/)
Nuno Gundar da Cruz (Insolvency)
(https://www.mlgts.pt/en/people/partners/Nuno-Gundar-da-Cruz/250/)

1 LOCAL ECONOMIC, POLITICAL AND CULTURAL ASPECTS

1.1 Country Profile

[01] Mainland Portugal is located in the south-westernmost point of continental Europe. Beyond its continental territory, Portugal integrates the Azores and Madeira archipelagos in the Atlantic Ocean.

[02] Due to its unique geographic location, Portugal is more than a country with a vast coastline, with more than five hundred beautiful sandy beaches, being commonly described as a gateway to Europe.

[03] Although the country offers good conditions for the production of renewable energy, it is still dependent on external energy, given that it has no fossil energy resources of its own. Consequently, it needs to import most of its primary energy consumption.[1]

[04] Portugal has interesting geological resources, and although ornamental and industrial stones are still the primary source of exports in this sector, it is envisaged that the discovery of large reserves of lithium will bring exciting new opportunities in this sector.

[05] Forest, woodland and forest perimeters are key resources in the country's economy, and the country is also rich in spring waters and natural minerals, with thermal spas having gained traction in recent decades.

[06] As of 31 December 2021, Portugal's estimated resident population was 10 352 042. This result translated into a negative effective growth rate of -0.19% as a result of net migration of 25,642 people.

[07] In 2021, the active population amounted to 5,151.1 thousand people, corresponding to an activity rate (fifteen years and over) of 59.2%. In 2021, the number of employees stood at 84.5% of the total employed population, of whom 83.1% had permanent contracts.

[08] According to the data from the Lists of Personnel (of the Ministry of Labour, Solidarity and Social Security), in 2020, the average monthly (gross) earnings of employees in Portugal amounted to EUR1 247.21. For 2022, the national minimum wage is set at EUR705.00.

[09] Of the multiple schemes comprising the Portuguese social protection system, Social Security is the most relevant.

[10] Income distribution remained characterised by strong inequality, although this has been declining since 2014. In 2020, the Gini coefficient was 33.0%, while according to the S80/S20 ratio, the equivalent net monetary income of the 20% of

---

1 '*Instituto Nacional de Estatística – Statistical Yearbook of Portugal: 2021*', Lisboa. INE, 2022. Available at Statistics Portugal –Web Portal (ine.pt). *All statistic information contained in this chapter is based on this report unless otherwise expressly stated.*

the population with the highest income was 5.7 times higher than the equivalent net monetary income of the 20% of the population with the lowest resources.

[11] According to the results of the 2015–2016 Household Budget Survey, the total annual mean consumption expenditure per household living in Portugal was EUR20 363.00. Together, the three main components of expenditure (i.e., housing, food, and transport) accounted for 60.3% of the total annual mean consumption of Portuguese-resident households in 2015–2016.

[12] Private consumption in 2021 increased by 4.5% in real terms (a 7.1% decrease in 2020). Public consumption increased by 4.1% (0.4% in 2020). It should be noted that in 2020 there was a negative impact on non-market production in volume caused by the measures adopted to reduce the spread of COVID-19, which implied the closure of several public services, particularly in the second quarter. In 2021, Gross Domestic Product (GDP) recorded a growth of 4.9% in volume, the highest since 1990, after the historic decrease of 8.4% in 2020, reflecting the markedly adverse effects of the COVID-19 pandemic on economic activity.

[13] In 2020, there were 1 301 000 non-financial enterprises in Portugal. The main economic indicators recorded a sharp decrease compared to 2019, with persons employed turnover, gross value added (GVA) and gross operating surplus (GOS) of non-financial enterprises down by 2.0%, 10.0% and 9.8%, respectively. By activity sector, the Information and Communication sector recorded the highest growth rates in the GVA (11.3%) and in turnover (7.0%). Despite a decrease of 6.1% compared to 2019, Industry continued to be the sector with the greatest weight in the GVA of non-financial enterprises (22.4%), which corresponded, in absolute terms, to EUR21.1 bn. The Accommodation and food services and Transport and Storage sectors were the most affected in the economic context experienced in 2020, with decreases in turnover of 40.8% and 24.3%, respectively, and in GVA of 53.9% and 33.9%, in the same order.

[14] The distribution by sector of activity was (i) trade: 215 033; (ii) agriculture and fishing: 126 907; (iii) construction and real estate activities: 144 268; (iv) accommodation and food service activities: 112 347; (v) industry: 67 492; (vi) transportation and storage: 34 237; (vii) information and communication: 21 312; (viii) energy and water: 6 172; and (ix) other services: 573 232. Enterprises with less than ten persons employed: 96.2%.

[15] In 2021, exports of goods increased by 18.3% in nominal terms compared to the previous year and amounted to EUR63 580 000 000.00. The evolution over the previous year, contrary to that seen in 2020 (-10.3%), reflects the increases in Intra-EU (+EUR7 090 m; corresponding to +18.5%) and Extra-EU exports (+EUR2 732 m; +17.8%). Spain, France, and Germany remained the main clients of national exports of goods, concentrating 50.9% of the total (+0.1 p.p. compared to 2020). Portugal exports mainly to Spain, France, Germany, the United Kingdom, the United States and Italy; and imports mainly from Spain, Germany, France, The Netherlands, Italy and China.

1.2 Governmental, Political and Legal System

[16] Portugal has been a democratic Republic since 1975. The Carnation Revolution (*Revolução dos Cravos*), which took place in 1974, was the movement that overthrew the dictatorial regime in Portugal of *Estado Novo* without resorting to violence.

[17] Alternation of different governing parties has taken place since 1975, and governmental stability is good.

[18] Portugal has been a member of the European Union (EU) since 1 January 1986 and is also part of the Eurozone (Euro Area).

[19] Portugal follows a civil law legal system where laws and decree-laws are approved by the Parliament and by the Government, respectively. Furthermore, the Azores and Madeira, as autonomous regions, are empowered to approve their own regional laws, local authorities may approve local regulations, and some administrative authorities, within the scope of their duties, may also approve regulations.

[20] The President of the Portuguese Republic, the Parliament, the Government and the Courts are the sovereign bodies in Portugal.

1.3 Current Economic Aspects

[21] The economic situation has been beneficial for M&A transactions in recent years, mainly due to (i) the European Central Bank's decision to keep interest rates low for a few more years; (ii) the availability of more financing options (whether equity financing, private equity, partnerships with family offices, funds, private or mixed placements or even traditional bank financing); (iii) strengthening balance sheets; (iv) the quality of some Portuguese assets; and (v) an exponential increase in private equity activity.

[22] In fact, demand from investors and from funds investing in private equity has had a marked effect on the Portuguese market, especially in relation to small- and medium-sized Iberian enterprises and in relation to the acquisition of controlling stakes in profitable companies that have never been listed. Going to the numbers and the deals, the volume of buyouts and growth transactions (i.e., more 'traditional' private equity) has decreased significantly compared to the previous year (the COVID-19 pandemic being often cited as its main reason). Until November 2021, private equity transactions represented a total volume of EUR2.169 bn, which represents a 68% drop compared to the same period in 2020. In venture capital, however, the market's upward trajectory has not been interrupted by the pandemic (rather to the contrary), and transaction volume actually increased by 87.6% compared to 2020 levels, rising to EUR1.542 bn.[2]

[2] TTR – Iberian Market Monthly Report, November 2021.

[23] There has been a significant increase in the demand for insurance for M&A transactions. W&I insurance is a high-premium product, and there is already a demand for tax, litigation and environmental and cyber contingencies insurance. Additionally, the increasing number and complexity of transactions have brought different solutions and mechanisms to determine a transaction's price by means of either a fixed price (locked-box mechanism) or an adjusted price dependent on the target company's performance (e.g., earn-outs) or valuations based on completion accounts. Depending on the characteristics of the different price adjustment models, some are usually seen as pro-buyer, while fixed-price models are usually favoured by sellers.

[24] It should be noted that despite the ability of the parties to subject their transaction documents to foreign law, especially when there are foreign investors involved, several M&A transactions involving Portuguese companies are subject to Portuguese law and jurisdiction. Furthermore, it is very common for disputes to be subject to foreign arbitration.

[25] Although the capital market is experiencing an increase in both IPO and secondary offers, it is still far from achieving its full potential. According to the Portuguese Securities Market Commission (*Comissão do Mercado de Valores Mobiliários*), the secondary market in January 2020 reached EUR2 480 000 000.00, a EUR604 700 000.00 (32.3%) increase from December 2019 and a EUR653 500 000.00 (35.8%) increase on January 2019. The Euronext Lisbon transaction value amounted to EUR2 313 000 000.00, representing an increase of 31.3% on a monthly basis and a 29.5% increase year on year. In 2019, about half of the Transactional Track Record's (TTR) total business was M&A, 20% venture capital, 20% asset acquisitions, and the other 10% involved private funds. By value, M&A transactions totalled EUR4 902 000 000.00, followed by asset acquisitions with EUR4 217 000 000.00, private fund operations with EUR3 913 000 000.00 and venture capital deals with EUR363 000 000.00.

1.4 Main Industries

[26] In 2021, according to the TTR, the Portuguese M&A market was the scene of 553 transactions, amounting in aggregate to EUR19 200 000 000.

[27] Technology is the most active sector, with 109 transactions, followed by the Real Estate sector, with 86 transactions, and the Finance and Insurance sector, with 62 transactions.

[28] As regards cross-border deal-making, in 2021, there were nearly 239 M&A transactions involving acquisitions of national companies by foreign entities. Spain remains the most active investor in Portugal, with the highest number of deals involving Portuguese companies, accounting for 63 transactions. Spain is followed by the United States, which accounted for 47 transactions, and France, with 28 transactions.

[29] In the outbound market, Portuguese companies' main targets were in Spain, with 31 transactions, and Brazil, with 8 transactions, followed by the United Kingdom, with 7 transactions.

[30] Although the Portuguese market is on an upward trajectory, there have been some fluctuations in investment values as well as in the sectors targeted.

[31] The number of transactions registered a 31% growth compared to the same period in 2020, as well as a 2% increase regarding the capital raised.

[32] According to data made available by TTR, Morais Leitão led the ranking of legal advisors by the number of transactions, with 24, having been among the most active legal advisors last year.

1.5 Cultural Aspects

[33] Portugal is internationally known as a safe and welcoming country. It is a great place to do business. Although somewhat bureaucratic, it is a developed country with a stable political system, offering the rule of law, freedom of speech and religion, and good infrastructure. It is also relatively cheap compared to other similar countries.

2 THE REGULATORY FRAMEWORK

2.1 Business Vehicles

[34] The Portuguese legal framework provides for the possibility of incorporation of four main types of commercial companies in Portugal, notably, (i) private limited liability companies by *quotas* (*sociedades por quotas*), typically for smaller companies which want a more flexible structure and fewer corporate government requirements; (ii) limited liability companies by shares (*sociedade anónima*) for larger companies, which can be private or publicly traded; (iii) *sociedades em nome coletivo* (partnerships, in which the partners are liable in an unlimited and subsidiary manner to the company and are jointly liable to the creditors); and (iv) *sociedades em comandita* (limited partnership); the last two of these being less common in typical M&A transactions.

[35] Under Portuguese law, each type of company follows a different set of rules when it comes to the relationship between the shareholders, including the terms of the liability regime and the type of organisation and duties involved. We therefore propose to outline the principal features of the regime applicable to the two principal vehicles used.

2.1.1 Private Limited Liability Companies by Quotas

[36] According to the Portuguese Companies Code (*Código das Sociedades Comerciais*) (PCC), a private limited liability company, by *quotas*, must be designated as such by using *Limitada* or the abbreviation *Lda.* The share capital is freely determined by the partners, and consequently, the minimum share capital may be as little as EUR2.00. The minimum number of partners in a limited liability company by *quotas* is two. However, it may be entirely owned by a sole partner provided it is incorporated as or converted into a wholly owned private limited liability company by *quotas* (*sociedade unipessoal por quotas*), in which case, the minimum share capital may amount to EUR1.00, and it will be subject to the legal rules governing this type of company.

[37] *Corporate bodies*: The Management Body is made up of one or more managers.

[38] The appointment of a supervisory body is not mandatory. However, if the company does not have a supervisory body, a statutory auditor must be appointed to carry out the statutory audit if two of the following three thresholds are exceeded for at least two consecutive years:

(i) balance sheet total: EUR1 500 000.00;
(ii) total of net sales and other income: EUR3 000 000.00;
(iii) average number of employees during the year: 50.

2.1.2 Limited Liability Companies by Shares

[39] A limited liability company by shares must be designated as such by using *Sociedade Anónima* or the abbreviation *S.A.*. Share limited liability companies must be incorporated by a sole corporate shareholder or by at least five shareholders and must have a minimum share capital of EUR50 000.00.

[40] *Corporate bodies*: For limited liability companies by shares, various structures are possible:

(i) A Board of Directors (or a Sole Director if the share capital does not exceed EUR200 000.00) and a Supervisory Board and a Statutory Auditor or a Sole Auditor (which must be a Statutory Auditor). However, a Supervisory Board must be established if:
   (a) the shares representing the company's share capital are admitted to trading on a regulated market;
   (b) the company is not wholly owned by another company adopting this structure, and two of the following three thresholds are exceeded for two consecutive years: (1) balance sheet total: EUR20 000 000.00; (2) net business volume: EUR40 000 000.00; (3) average number of employees during the year: 250.
(ii) a Board of Directors, which includes an Audit Committee and a Statutory Auditor; or

(iii) an Executive Board of Directors (or a Sole Director if the share capital does not exceed EUR200 000.00); a General and Supervisory Board and a Statutory Auditor.

2.1.3 Parent Company Liability

[41] Whenever a Portuguese company holds 100% of the share capital of another Portuguese company, these companies are, for the purposes of the PCC, in a group relationship to which specific rules apply, notably the following:

(i) Parent company liability for the liabilities of the subsidiary: the parent company is liable for all the latter's liabilities which have arisen before or after the acquisition of the whole domain until the ending of the group relationship. The parent company becomes liable following a period of thirty days from the date on which the subsidiary was regarded as being in default.

(ii) Parent company liability for the losses of the subsidiary: the parent company may be compelled by the subsidiary to cover the latter's annual losses if such losses are not covered by the reserves accrued during that same period. This liability is only enforceable once the group relationship has ended unless the subsidiary is declared insolvent.

2.1.4 Formalities

[42] Several facts are subject to registration with the Commercial Registry Office, such as: (i) incorporation; (ii) any resolution of the general meeting for the acquisition of assets by the company, if legally required; (iii) the unification, split and transfer of *quotas*; (iv) any promise of disposal or encumbrance of *quotas*, and in some cases, pre-emption agreements affecting such quotas; (v) the creation and transfer of usufruct, pledge, arrest, attachment and seizure in criminal proceedings of *quotas* or rights over them, as well as any other acts or measures affecting their free disposal; (vi) the amortisation of *quotas* and the exclusion and resignation of partners; (vii) resolutions for the redemption, conversion or remission of shares; (viii) the appointment and termination of duties, for any reason other than expiry of the fixed term, of members of the company's management and supervisory bodies, as well as the company secretary (when applicable); (ix) the submission of accounts; (x) the change of the registered office of the company or the transfer of the registered office abroad; (xi) the draft terms of any internal or cross-border merger and the draft terms of any demerger of companies; (xii) the extension, internal or cross-border merger, demerger, transformation and winding up of companies, as well as any increase, reduction or reintegration of the capital and any other amendment to the articles of association; (xiii) completion of the liquidation (or of the return to business) of the company; (xiv) any decision to maintain total control of one company by another, in a group relationship, as well as the termination of that control; and (xv) any contract of subordination, its amendments and its termination.

[43] Shareholders' resolutions of limited liability companies by shares are generally approved by a majority of the votes cast, irrespective of the percentage of share capital represented at the meeting (unless otherwise required by law or by the articles of association). However, certain matters must be passed, notably at the first convening of the meeting, by two-thirds of the votes cast (e.g., amendments of the articles of association, merger, demerger, transformation and dissolution).

[44] The regime applicable to shareholders' resolutions of limited liability companies by shares generally applies also to partners' resolutions of limited companies by *quotas* unless specified as applicable only to limited liability companies by shares.

2.2 Laws Affecting M&A

[45] Without prejudice to certain special laws applying to State-owned companies (when applicable), the general legal framework for M&A activity is established by the Civil Code (*Código Civil*), enacted by Decree-Law No. 44/344, of 25 November, as amended, the Commercial Code (*Código Comercial*), enacted by Letter of Law of 28 June 1888, as amended, and the PCC, enacted by Decree-Law No. 262/86 of 2 September, as amended, along with ancillary legislation and regulations.

[46] As regards transactions involving companies with shares admitted to trading on a regulated market, the key provisions are set out in the Portuguese Securities Code (*Código dos Valores Mobiliários*) (PSC), enacted by Decree-Law No. 486/99, of 13 November, as amended.

[47] The Portuguese Insolvency and Companies Recovery Code (*Código da Insolvência e da Recuperação de Empresas*) (PIC), enacted by Decree-Law No. 53/2004 of 18 March, as amended, could also be crucial when assessing a specific deal involving insolvency or company restructuring proceedings.

[48] Additionally, for transactions in regulated sectors, specific laws and regulations are also applicable, as explained below. Other areas of law that play an important role in structuring the transaction or in the due diligence phase are labour law (e.g., the protection granted to employees in a transfer of undertakings), tax and competition (merger control).

[49] Although the Portuguese legal system is based on civil law, common law jurisdictions can also have a significant influence on cross-border transactions. Regulation (EC) No. 593/2008 (Rome I), of the European Parliament and of the Council, of 17 June 2008, as well as Regulation (EU) No. 1215/212, of the European Parliament and of the Council, of 12 December 2012, which are effective in Portugal, grant the parties to a civil or commercial contract the right to choose its governing law and jurisdiction, provided that any mandatory rules established under local law are complied with (e.g., provisions governing the transfer of shares, assignment of credits and obligations). Although, following Brexit, Regulation (EU) No. 1215/212, of the European Parliament and of the Council, of 12 December 2012 is no longer applicable to proceedings commenced after 31 December 2020 where parties have chosen the jurisdiction of English courts, the European Union, including

Portugal, is also party to the 2005 Hague Convention on Choice of Court Agreements. Thus, the parties can, subject to the applicable requisites and limitations, opt to submit the transaction documents to a foreign law and jurisdiction, especially when foreign investors are involved, even though several deals affecting Portuguese companies remain subject to Portuguese law. Foreign investors must be prepared for a number of specific procedures.

[50] In Portugal, the acquisition structure of an M&A transaction depends on several aspects, such as: (i) the type of business carried on by the target company; (ii) the buyer's capacity to fund the acquisition; (iii) the purpose(s) of the transaction, its risks and liabilities; (iv) the legal and tax considerations affecting the target company to be acquired; and (v) the target's financial condition. The most common means of acquisition regarding private companies are (i) share deals; (ii) asset deals; (iii) the transfer of a business as a going concern; and (iv) mergers.

[51] Mergers involve specific procedures and the preparation of mandatory documentation such as the merger project, a statutory auditor's report and the approval of the merger project by the shareholders of each of the companies concerned.

[52] Two or more companies, even if of different types, may merge into one, and this may be carried out by any one of the following:

(i) *Merger by concentration*: through the global transfer of the assets of one or more companies to another company and the attribution to the shareholders of the former of parts, shares or *quotas* of the latter.
(ii) *Merger by incorporation of a new company*: by means of the incorporation of a new company, to which the assets of the merged companies are globally transferred, with parts, shares or quotas of the new company being attributed to the holders of the parts, shares or quotas of the merged companies.

[53] In addition to the parts, shares or *quotas* of the acquiring company or of the new company, shareholders of the merged company or companies may be granted amounts of money not exceeding 10% of the nominal value of their participation.

[54] Dissolved companies may merge with other companies, whether dissolved or not, even if the liquidation is performed judicially, provided that they meet the requirements for the return of the company to trading (in accordance with its purpose).

[55] A company may not merge from the date of the petition to file for insolvency or from the date of the request for declaration of insolvency.

[56] In the case of mergers by concentration of a company by another which holds at least 90% of its capital, minority shareholders may only (in the absence of a special provision in the articles of association) exercise a right of withdrawal when they vote against the merger project in the General Meeting of Shareholders.

[57] In a demerger, a company is allowed to:

(i) assign part of its assets to a new company;
(ii) dissolve and divide its assets, each of the resulting parts being intended to incorporate a new company;

(iii) separate parts of its assets, or to dissolve itself, dividing its assets into two or more parts, in order to merge them with existing companies or with parts of the assets of other companies which have been separated by identical processes and for the same purpose.

[58] The companies resulting from the demerger may be of a different type from the demerged company.

2.3 Relevant Regulatory Authorities

[59] The main regulatory bodies that govern M&A transactions are (i) the Portuguese Competition Authority (*Autoridade da Concorrência*) (AdC); (ii) the Portuguese Securities Market Commission (*Comissão do Mercado de Valores Mobiliários*) (CMVM); (iii) the Bank of Portugal (*Banco de Portugal*) (BdP); (iv) the Insurance and Pension Fund Supervision Authority (*Autoridade de Supervisão de Seguros e Fundos de Pensões*) (ASF); (v) the National Authority for Communications (ANACOM); (vi) the Energy Services Regulatory Authority (*Entidade Reguladora dos Serviços Energéticos*) (ERSE); and (vii) the Media Regulator (*Entidade Reguladora para a Comunicação Social*) (ERC). Depending on the target and the relevant sector of activity, other laws and regulations may also apply.

2.3.1 AdC

[60] AdC is an independent administrative body created in 2003, with powers across the whole Portuguese economy for the application of competition rules in coordination with sectoral regulatory bodies. The key economic sectors under the AdC's close scrutiny include: Banking, Financial Markets and Insurance, Telecommunications and Media, Energy and Fuels, Health and Pharmaceuticals, Education, Distribution and Food, Environment and Waste Management, Liberal Professions, Transport and Infrastructures, and Construction. Since the beginning of 2018, the AdC has had direct and full access to all the information available on the Public Procurement Portal (BASE portal) and the Public Works Observatory (*Observatório das Obras Públicas*). This is expected to facilitate the detection of anticompetitive practices in public procurement.

[61] Its mission is to ensure the application of the rules for the promotion and defence of competition in the private, public, cooperative and social sectors, in compliance with the principles of a market economy and free competition, with a view to the efficient functioning of the markets, the optimum allocation of resources and the interests of consumers, in accordance with its by-laws, as approved by Decree-Law No. 125/2014, of 18 August, amended lastly by Law No. 17/2022, of 17 August. As regards merger control, the AdC pays special attention to non-notified mergers implemented without its prior approval.

[62] In order to accomplish its mission, the AdC has the following delegated powers and authorities: (i) to ensure compliance with the laws, regulations and decisions of national and EU law aimed at promoting and defending competition; (ii) to encourage the adoption of practices that promote competition and a competition culture among economic agents and the general public; (iii) to give priority to the treatment of issues that it is called upon to examine, as provided for in the competition legal regime; (iv) to disseminate, in particular to economic operators, guidelines considered relevant for competition policy; (v) to monitor the activity and establish cooperative relations with EU institutions, national, foreign and international entities and bodies with attributions in the competition area; (vi) to promote research on the promotion and defence of competition, developing initiatives and establishing association or cooperation protocols with public or private entities that prove to be appropriate for this purpose; (vii) to contribute to the improvement of the Portuguese regulatory system in all areas that may affect free competition, whether on its own initiative or at the request of the Assembly of the Republic or the Government; (viii) to exercise all powers that EU law confers on national competition authorities in the field of competition rules applicable to undertakings; (ix) to ensure, without prejudice to the powers of the Ministry of Foreign Affairs, the technical representation of the Portuguese State in EU or international bodies in matters of competition policy; and (x) to exercise any other powers legally or statutorily conferred upon it.

[63] In order to carry out its duties, the AdC has sanctioning, supervisory and regulatory powers, which may be summarised as follows:

- (i) In the exercise of its sanctioning powers:
  - (a) to identify and investigate conduct likely to infringe national and EU competition law, in particular with regard to practices restricting competition and the control of concentrations between undertakings; to investigate and decide on the respective cases;
  - (b) to impose fines and other sanctions and measures provided for by law; and
  - (c) to adopt interim measures in accordance with the competition law and other applicable legal provisions.
- (ii) In the exercise of its supervisory powers:
  - (a) to instruct and decide administrative procedures concerning concentration operations of companies subject to prior notification;
  - (b) to carry out studies, inspections and audits that may be necessary in competition matters; and
  - (c) to carry out other acts provided by law.
- (iii) In the exercise of its regulatory powers:
  - (a) to prepare and approve regulations and other rules of a general nature and instructions or other rules of a particular nature, as provided for by law;
  - (b) to issue recommendations and generic directives;
  - (c) at the request of the Assembly of the Republic or of the Government, to pronounce its views on legislative or other initiatives concerning the promotion and defence of competition; and
  - (d) to formulate suggestions or proposals for the creation or revision of the legal and regulatory framework.

[64] Under the Competition Act (Law No. 19/2012, of 8 May, amended lastly by Law No. 17/2022, of 17 August), AdC has exclusive competence to assess and decide on concentrations subject to mandatory notification. However, a concentration which is prohibited by AdC may still be approved by the Council of Ministers subject to commitments, pursuant to an extraordinary (and seldom-used) appeal procedure. All decisions issued by AdC can also be challenged in the Competition, Supervision and Regulation Court.

2.3.2 CMVM

[65] CMVM is a public legal entity with administrative and financial autonomy and its own assets. Established in May 1991 (by the Decree-Law No. 142-A/91 of 10 April), CMVM is tasked with supervising and regulating the financial instruments markets as well as agents operating within those markets and with promoting investor protection. CMVM has regulation, regulatory, supervisory, oversight and infraction sanctioning powers. CMVM is part of the European System of Financial Supervision and of the National Council of Financial Supervisors.

[66] The CMVM also has the following responsibilities:

(i) to sanction breaches of the PSC and of supplementary legislation;
(ii) to ensure the stability of financial markets by contributing to the identification and prevention of systemic risk;
(iii) to contribute to the development of the financial instrument markets;
(iv) to provide information and handle complaints from retail investors;
(v) to mediate conflicts between entities subject to its supervision and between them and investors;
(vi) to assist the Government and its members responsible for Finance;
(vii) to perform any other duties assigned to it by law.

[67] The following persons and entities are subject to supervision by the CMVM:

(i) securities issuers;
(ii) financial intermediaries;
(iii) independent consultants;
(iv) entities managing markets, settlement systems and centralised securities systems, and entities whose purpose is to clear transactions in commodity derivatives markets;
(v) professional investors;
(vi) investment funds;
(vii) holders of qualifying holdings in companies with securities admitted to trading on a regulated market;
(viii) guarantee funds, investor compensation schemes and their management entities;
(ix) auditors and credit rating companies;
(x) funds and venture capital companies;
(xi) funds and securitisation companies and securitisation fund management companies; and

(xii) other persons who carry out securities-related activities in a professional or ancillary capacity.

[68] CMVM must be informed in advance of operations concerning companies under the provisions of the PSC. Pursuant to this Code, transactions involving public bids must also be registered in advance with, and are subject to a formal approval by, the securities regulator.

2.3.3 BdP

[69] BdP is the central bank of the Portuguese Republic, and it is a part of the European System of Central Banks (ESCB), the Single Supervisory Mechanism and the Single Resolution Mechanism.

[70] Any natural or legal person who, directly or indirectly, intends to hold a qualifying shareholding in a credit institution or financial institution must notify BdP in advance of its project. A qualifying holding is any direct or indirect holding corresponding to at least 10% of the capital or voting rights in a credit institution or financial institution or which, for whatever reason, makes it possible to exercise a significant influence over the management of the credit institution or financial institution. The BdP must also be notified in advance of any acts involving an increase in a qualifying shareholding whenever such acts may result in a percentage reaching or exceeding any of the thresholds of 10%, 20%, one-third or 50% of the capital or voting rights of the institution in which the holding is held, or when the latter becomes a subsidiary of the acquiring entity. The notification must be made whenever the initiative or set of initiatives envisaged by the person/entity concerned may result in any of the situations indicated, even if the result is not guaranteed in advance. Furthermore, BdP must be informed of any acts or facts resulting in the acquisition of a shareholding of at least 5% of the share capital or voting rights of a credit institution or financial institution within fifteen days from the occurrence of such acts or fact. In such case, if the BdP considers that the holding in question corresponds to a qualifying shareholding, it must inform the proposed acquirer within thirty days. The BdP may also, at any time, declare that a holding is a qualifying shareholding whenever it gains knowledge of certain acts or facts in relation to which communication to BdP was omitted or wrongly made or that may alter the influence exercised by the holder over the institution's administration.

[71] The intention to cease holding or to decrease a participation below a threshold of 20%, one-third or 50%, in a credit institution or in a financial institution, or in such a way that the institution ceases to be a subsidiary, must be notified in advance to BdP with the new amount of the relevant participation. If a qualifying holding decreases below a 5% threshold, BdP will inform the holder whether it considers that the shareholding in question is a qualifying holding.

[72] The merger of credit institutions, whether among themselves or with financial companies, as well as their demerger, depends on the prior authorisation of BdP.

[73] Shareholders' agreements between credit institutions regarding the exercise of voting rights are subject to registration with BdP under penalty of ineffectiveness.

[74] It should also be noted that credit institutions are prevented from holding, directly or indirectly, more than 25% of the voting rights of a commercial company for one continuous period (or interpolated periods) totalling three years and five years if held through a risk capital fund or a holding company. Exceptions apply to shareholdings by a credit institution in other credit institutions, financial companies, financial institutions, ancillary services companies, securitisation companies, insurance companies, subsidiaries of insurance companies held in accordance with the law applicable to them, insurance brokers and insurance intermediaries, pension fund management companies, venture capital companies and holding companies which only hold shares in the companies mentioned above, as well as to shareholdings by credit institutions in real estate investment funds for rental housing and real estate investment companies.

2.3.4 ASF

[75] ASF's mission is to ensure the proper functioning of the insurance market and pension funds in Portugal in order to contribute to the protection of policyholders, insured persons, participants and beneficiaries. This mission is ensured by promoting the stability and financial soundness of all institutions under its supervision, as well as ensuring the maintenance of high standards of conduct by operators.

[76] ASF has regulatory, authorisation or non-opposition powers, registration or certification, on-site and off-site supervision, enforcement, revocation, misdemeanour and institutional powers.

[77] The intention to acquire or strengthen a qualified shareholding (10%, 20%, one-third, or 50%) in an insurance company must be notified in advance to the ASF, under Law No. 147/2015, of 9 September, as amended, which may oppose the operation if it considers that prudent management of the target company cannot be ensured. Furthermore, the intention to acquire a shareholding enabling a significant management influence to be exercised in the target company must be notified in advance to ASF.

2.3.5 ERC

[78] ERC regulates the media sector in Portugal and exercises the necessary regulatory and supervisory functions which are vested in it by the Constitution, the Law and its By-laws (Law No. 53/2005 of 8 November).

[79] All entities under the jurisdiction of the Portuguese State carrying out media activities are subject to ERC supervision. The universe of regulated entities includes, *inter alia*, news agencies, radio and television operators or entities editing periodical publications (irrespective of the means of distribution used).

[80] According to Law No. 78/2015 of 29 July, the following facts in relation to any entity under ERC supervision must be reported within ten working days of its occurrence:

(i) acquisition (or exceeding), by a holder, of 5%, 10%, 20%, 30%, 40% or 50% of the share capital or voting rights;
(ii) acquisition (or exceeding) by any entity in the chain to which a shareholding of at least 5% must be attributed, of the thresholds of 5%, 10%, 20%, 30%, 40% or 50% of the share capital or voting rights;
(iii) a reduction by a holder of his shareholding below each of the percentages indicated in the preceding subparagraphs;
(iv) a change in the ownership of the entity pursuing media activities;
(v) a change in the composition of the management bodies or in the structure of responsibility for the guidance and supervision of the contents broadcasted; and
(vi) a change in the shareholdings by the holders of entities pursuing media activities, in legal persons holding direct or indirect shareholdings in other media.

[81] As a further note, shareholders' agreements aimed at acquiring, maintaining or reinforcing a qualified shareholding in an entity pursuing media activities must be reported to the ERC within ten working days of their conclusion. Under certain conditions, ERC is entitled to publish such shareholders' agreements.

2.4 Controls/Restrictions on Foreign Investment

[82] Although foreign investment in Portugal is not restricted, there are some sectors where government authorisation is required to proceed with such investment. These areas include sectors that are typically regulated, namely telecommunications and media, but also the defence sector.

2.4.1 Defence

[83] First, in the defence sector, the authorisation and supervision of industry, trade and intermediation of goods and military technologies are under the responsibility of the Ministry of National Defence, in particular the Directorate General of National Defence Resources (*Direção-Geral de Recursos da Defesa Nacional*) (DGNDR), with the aim of ensuring that these activities are in line with the strategic interests of the Country and its various international commitments.

[84] In this regard, it should be noted that Portugal is a contracting party to several conventions and agreements, such as the Chemical Weapons Convention or the Wassenaar Arrangement on Export Controls for Conventional Arms and Dual-Use Goods and Technologies. Furthermore, as a Member State of the EU, Portugal is also bound to comply with EU Community principles and guidelines.

[85] The trade and industry of goods and military technology is governed by Law No. 49/2009 of 5 August, and these activities are subject to certain authorisations and conditions. These activities may be carried out by companies incorporated under Portuguese law but also by natural or legal persons authorised to trade in goods and military technology in other Member States.

[86] The exercise of these activities by commercial companies incorporated in Portugal is subject to a licence from the Minister of National Defence. To that end, the interested parties must submit an application to the Minister of National Defence, namely to the DGRDN, in which they must identify not only the specific activity they intend to carry out but also the military goods and technologies in question, their partners, directors or managers, as well as the markets that the company intends to target, but also make available their By-laws and other legal and commercial information.

[87] The granting of the licence is subject to the cumulative verification of various criteria and will not be granted to those companies or individuals who have been convicted of crimes of bankruptcy, falsification, fraud, corruption or who have been involved in illicit arms trading.

[88] The trade-in goods and military technology in Portugal by entities authorised to carry out those activities in other European Union Member States depends solely on prior registration in the DGNDR database.

[89] Furthermore, it should be noted that the export of goods and military technology and the import of raw materials and/or other goods to manufacture such equipment is also subject to prior registration.

2.4.2 Banking and Financial Services

[90] In respect of banking and financial activities, we note that this is a regulated sector in Portugal and banking and financial activities can only be carried out by credit institutions or financial companies that have been previously authorised.

[91] In addition, foreign investment in credit institutions and financial companies can be seen as being subject to previous authorisation that may have occurred in the context of the assessment of a potential acquisition of a qualifying holding in a credit institution or financial company (please *see* above in the section headed 'Relevant Regulatory Authorities' for further details).

2.4.3 Communications

[92] With respect to the telecommunications sector, the provision of electronic communications depends on general authorisation by the regulatory authority, ANACOM, which also performs supervisory, audit and sanctioning functions.

[93] The legal framework is established by Law No. 5/2004, of 10 February, which transposed into Portuguese law Directives No. 2002/19/EC, 2002/20/EC, 2002/21/EC and 2002/22/EC and which determines that although the provision of electronic communications networks and services is subject to the general authorisation regime, it is not dependent on any prior decision or act by ANACOM, which should proceed to its registration.

[94] Therefore companies wishing to offer electronic communications networks and services in Portugal are only required to communicate this in advance to ANACOM, with a brief description of the network or service they intend to offer and to indicate the date envisaged for the beginning of their activity. Once this communication has been made, the companies may immediately begin operations, despite the constraints arising from the allocation of rights of use of frequencies and numbers, these being dependent on request and being allocated, as a rule, for a renewable period of fifteen years.

[95] In the media sector, we will address some of the aspects that may be relevant in the decision to invest in Portugal, especially any authorisations that may be required in the radio and television sectors, whose regimes are very similar. Both sectors are regulated by ERC.

[96] Access to and the exercise of television activity is subject to registration and licence granted by the ERC through a public tender, opened by the decision of the Government. These licences and authorisations are generally issued for a period of fifteen years, renewable for equal periods. They are granted to a specific entity, are non-transferable and are conditional on the provision of those services throughout the national territory, including the autonomous regions (Madeira and the Azores).

[97] This activity is regulated by the Television Act (Law No. 27/2007, of 30 July), which applies to parties carrying on television activities under Portuguese jurisdiction. In order to develop that activity, companies must include the exercise of the television activity in their corporate purpose and must have the minimum share capital set out in that Act, the amount of which depends on the service and coverage offered.

[98] This activity must comply with the competition rules, and the legal framework prevents it from being exercised or financed, directly or indirectly, by political parties or by associations, trade union organisations, or public associations, except if it is exercised exclusively through the Internet or refers to conditional access channels.

[99] Turning now to the radio sector, which is governed by the Radio Law (Law No. 54/2010 of 24 December), we should note that the access and exercise of this activity are subject to licensing granted by the ERC, generally for fifteen years, renewable, through public tender or authorisation, depending on whether or not the programme services to be provided use the terrestrial broadcasting spectrum.

[100] Radioactivity consisting only of broadcasting of programme services over the Internet does not require prior authorisation and is solely subject to registration.

[101] This activity must also comply with the competition rules and can only be exercised by legal persons whose corporate purpose is the exercise of such activity, although associations or foundations that pursue humanitarian, educational, cultural, scientific or student or social purposes are excluded from this limitation. As in the television sector, this activity may not be exercised or financed by political parties or organisations.

2.4.4 Construction/Planning

[102] An additional matter that we would like to highlight is existing planning permissions since it is very likely that carrying out an investment in Portugal will have urban planning implications.

[103] In Portugal, as in other countries in the EU, the construction of buildings, regardless of their ultimately intended use (whether residential, commercial, services, tourism, industry, etc.), as well as allotment operations or urbanisation works, are subject to the provisions set out in land use plans and subject to prior control from the competent public authorities, through administrative licensing procedures.

[104] Allotment operations are those in which the developer of a given land area divides or restructures it to create plots intended for the construction of buildings. The allotment operations are approved by the competent municipality. Once approved, the allotment licence is issued, setting out urban parameters for each plot, such as the area of the plot, the construction area, the number of floors, height and construction footprint.

[105] Urbanisation works are construction works intended to create or renovate infrastructures which serve buildings and urban spaces, such as public roads, sidewalks, sewage systems, water, power and gas supply and also green spaces and other public use spaces. Usually, these urbanisation works are linked to the approval of allotments in order to create the necessary infrastructures that will allow for the construction of buildings. It is also possible to have urbanisation works that are not included in allotment operations.

[106] Lastly, we have construction licences for the construction of buildings. Depending on the specific location and the specific framework applicable to the land or site, construction may depend only on a prior communication to the competent municipality, consisting of a statement presented by the promoter, together with all of the mandatory and other relevant documents required. Once this prior communication has been presented, the municipality has only to check, within eight business days, whether all of the relevant documents have been submitted. If they have, the promoter then has only to pay the administrative fees, and construction may begin.

2.4.5 Other Sectors

[107] In addition to the above, it should be noted that reporting obligations for administrative and statistical purposes may apply and that in certain regulated sectors – such as banking, insurance, infrastructure and transportation – the acquisition of a qualifying shareholding may be subject to prior approval and/or notification of the relevant regulators.

[108] In particular, Decree-Law No. 138/2014 of 15 September establishes rules on the safeguarding of strategic assets and applies to the main infrastructure and assets for defence and natural security, as well as to the provision of essential services in the energy, transport and communications sectors.

[109] Pursuant to that Decree-Law, the Government may oppose the acquisition of control over a strategic asset by a person or company of a third country to the EU or the European Economic Area (EEA) if such acquisition poses a genuine and sufficiently serious threat to national security or to the security of supply of the relevant essential services. That Decree-Law specifies the situations where a genuine threat may arise (such as connections of the person or company to a terrorist group) and establishes a review and opposition procedure.

[110] The Government may initiate an evaluation procedure within thirty working days of the conclusion of any legal transaction which results, directly or indirectly, in the acquisition of control, directly or indirectly, by a person or persons from third countries to the EU and the EEA, over strategic assets, irrespective of their legal form (or from the date on which such transaction became generally known, if later), in order to evaluate the risk of such operation for national defence and security or for the security of supply of the country in services fundamental to the national interest. If an evaluation is initiated, the acquiring person or persons must submit the relevant information and documents about the operation to the Government. In a sixty-day period counting from the complete delivery of the relevant information and documents, the Council of Ministers (*Conselho de Ministros*) may decide to oppose the operation through a reasoned decision, and in compliance with applicable legal rules and principles, in particular the principle of proportionality. The absence of a decision within this period is deemed to serve as a non-opposition decision. If an opposition decision is adopted, all acts and legal transactions relating to the transaction are null and void, including those concerning economic exploitation or the exercise of rights over assets or the entities that control them. This decision may be challenged in accordance with the Code of Procedure in Administrative Courts (*Código de Processo nos Tribunais Administrativos*).

[111] Acquirers of assets covered by the law may request the Government to confirm that it does not plan to oppose the transaction. Confirmation is tacitly given if no investigation is initiated by the Government within thirty working days.

2.5 Incentives for Foreign Investment

2.5.1 Incentives/Free Trade Zone

[112] Portugal boasts several incentives for foreign investment, such as productive investment, job creation incentives, research and development (R&D), the so-called Golden Visa and a non-habitual resident regime (the latter two for individuals). Notable sector-specific incentives include those aimed at capital markets, the financial sector in general, real estate development and rehabilitation, the shipping industry, wine production, sports and cultural activities, cinema, forestry

management, patronage, philanthropic activities and the cooperative sector. Tax incentives for foreign investment tend to translate into reductions or partial/full exemptions from many state and local taxes (e.g., pension funds, collective investment vehicles, exemptions applicable to foreign financial institutions and debt instruments).

[113] Additionally, Portugal has one free trade zone in Madeira (the International Business Centre of Madeira), which offers special investment incentives and an attractive tax framework and low operating costs provided for in the current regime IV, but without being deemed a tax haven either by the Organisation for Economic Co-operation and Development (OECD) or by the EU, having been authorised by the European Commission as legal regional State Aid.

2.5.2 Nationalisation and Expropriation

[114] Nationalisations and expropriations are constitutionally authorised in cases of public interest and against payment of compensation. They are respectively ruled by Law No. 62-A/2008, of 11 November, and by the Expropriations Code (*Código das Expropriações*) (Law No. 168/99, of 18 September).

[115] Public appropriation of a company's shares through nationalisation is possible when, for exceptional and especially justified reasons, it is deemed necessary to safeguard the public interest. If the company in question is admitted to trading on a regulated market, the management entity must suspend the trading of all the shares from the moment the nationalisation is announced.

[116] The right to compensation is granted to the holders of the company's shares, as well as to any holders of encumbrances or charges levied on them. Its value is appraised by at least two independent entities in accordance with the company's assets and financial situation on the date of entry into force of the act of nationalisation.

[117] With regard to expropriation on the grounds of public utility: it is possible to appropriate immovable property and the rights inherent to it on the grounds of public utility and against the payment of a justified compensation. Nevertheless, before requesting the declaration of public utility, the expropriating entity must endeavour to acquire the assets directly on the basis of normal private law procedures.

[118] Thus, the expropriation procedure could end in one of two ways: (i) an amicable expropriation, by which the expropriating entity succeeds in reaching an agreement with the owner for the purchase of the asset; or (ii) a litigious expropriation whereby, in the absence of agreement on the amount of compensation, the amount will be established through arbitration, with the possibility of recourse of that decision to the judicial courts.

2.5.3 Financing Options

[119] The common financing options in Portugal for acquisitions include bilateral loans and syndicated lending (either domestic or cross-border).

[120] In recent years, there has also been an increase in the use of bond facilities, and private equity and venture capital funds have been more active. Domestic banks typically undertake lending for large-scale investments on a syndicated basis.

[121] There are no differences in the rules (as between a domestic and a foreign lender) for the taking of security over local immovable property.

2.5.4 Entry and Exit of Capital/Foreign Bank Accounts

[122] In general terms and without prejudice to anti-money laundering and prevention of terrorist financing laws, there are no restrictions on the entry and exit of capital in Portugal, except in the case of cash controls applicable in the EU (Decree-Law No. 61/2007 of 14 March, executing the provisions of Regulation (EU) No. 2018/1672 on controls on cash entering or leaving the Union). The same principle applies to the transfer of funds to foreign lenders in respect of interest payments.

[123] In Portugal, it is not illegal to open a bank account in a country other than the one in which the holder is located, but any income received from it, or in it, must be declared to the competent tax authorities.

[124] With regard to foreign exchange, there are no exchange controls or currency regulations impeding foreign investors, or hindering inbound and outbound investments, provided that the rules regarding prevention of money laundering and financing of terrorism are observed.

2.6 Specific Issues of Company/Securities Law

2.6.1 Levels of Approval

[125] The need for and levels of approval required can vary according to the type of M&A transaction. However, in general, the following principles need to be taken into account:

(i) in share deals in which the target is a limited liability company by *quotas*, the assignment of *quotas* is subject to the consent of the company, to be granted by the majority of its partners, except if the articles of association expressly waive such consent. In any event, the assignment does not become effective vis-à-vis the company until it has been communicated to the company. However, the articles of association can forbid the assignment and/or include a pre-emption right in favour of the other partners in relation to the transfer of *quotas* to third parties, this latter being relatively common for this type of company;

(ii) in share deals involving a limited liability company by shares as the target, the general principle is free transferability. Nevertheless, although the articles of association and shareholders' agreements may not exclude the transferability of shares, they may establish limits to it, such as pre-emptive rights, the consent of the company, and any such limits have to be assessed on a case-by-case basis;

(iii) in the case of mergers, and in the absence of any special provisions in the articles of association, the decision must be taken in accordance with the terms prescribed for amendments of the articles of association. These terms require favourable votes (i) by at least three-quarters of the share capital for a private limited liability company for *quotas*; and (ii) in the case of a limited liability company by shares, by (a) at least two-thirds of the votes cast (*quórum deliberativo*), provided that at least one-third of the share capital is represented at the General Meeting, on the first call, or regardless of the percentage of the share capital represented on the second call (*quórum constitutivo*), or (b) on the second call, by a majority of the votes cast (*quórum deliberativo*), if at least half of the share capital is represented (*quórum constitutivo*). However, the specific consent of certain shareholders might be needed (failing which the merger will not be registered by the Commercial Registry Office) if the merger:
   (a) increases the obligations and liabilities of all or some of the shareholders;
   (b) affects special rights held by some of the shareholders;
   (c) alters the proportion of their shareholdings in relation to other shareholders of the same company, except to the extent that such alteration results from payments that are required to comply with legal provisions imposing a minimum or fixed value on each unit of participation; and also
   (d) if any of the participating companies have different categories of shares, the merger resolutions of the respective general meetings can only take effect following approval by the special meeting of each such category.

[126] Within one month of publication of the registration of the merger project, creditors of participating companies whose claims predate such publication may submit a judicial opposition to the merger on the grounds of the damage that such merger may cause to their rights, provided that they have requested the company to satisfy their claim or to provide an appropriate guarantee, for at least fifteen days previously, without success.

[127] If the company/companies to be merged has/have bonds outstanding, bondholders' meetings of each company must be held to allow the bondholders to express their opinion about any potential damage the merger may cause them. Resolutions are passed by an absolute majority of the bondholders present and represented.

[128] Thus, the entry into a typical share deal (i) by a limited company by *quotas* is, in general, subject to the approval of its partners; (ii) by a limited company by shares is generally subject to the approval of its board of directors; and (iii) in the case of mergers are subject to approval of the shareholders of the companies concerned, regardless of their type.

[129] Other consents may be needed for certain transactions, such as consents from regulators, financing entities or suppliers, particularly in the case of change of control provisions.

2.6.2 Form of Consideration

[130] The parties are free to choose between offering a cash consideration or other types of consideration. However, in the majority of M&A transactions, specific tax considerations must be taken into account in this respect.

[131] In general, parties are free to negotiate and offer different terms to different shareholders of a target company, but with some exceptions (particularly in the case of public takeovers).

2.6.3 Security

[132] The provision of real or personal guarantees of the obligations of other entities is regarded as contrary to the corporate purpose of the providing company unless there is a justified self-interest of the guaranteeing company or it is a company in a control or group relationship.

[133] As a general principle, a company may not grant loans or in any way provide funds or guarantees to enable a third party to subscribe for or otherwise acquire shares in its own capital. However, this is not applicable to transactions that are part of the current operations of banks or other financial institutions, nor to transactions carried out with a view to the acquisition of shares by or for the staff of the company (or of an associated company), provided that such transactions do not result in the net assets of the company becoming less than the amount of the subscribed capital plus those reserves whose distribution is not allowed by law or by the articles of association. Any agreements or unilateral acts which contravene these requirements are null and void.

[134] In general, the shareholders of a company are not precluded from providing real or personal guarantees in its favour.

[135] A facility agreement secured by a mortgage is the most common form of financing and security for real estate projects. The loan-to-value ratio ranges between 65% and 80% of the value of the commercial property granted as security.

[136] As a general rule, no governmental or other consent is required for the provision of security. Nonetheless, there are certain specific assets, such as assets in the public domain or linked to public services, over which security cannot be granted. This depends on a specific analysis of the assets in question.

[137] Under Portuguese law, the concept of a floating charge or a general charge over all the assets of a company is not recognised.

[138] Common forms of security include:

(i) Mortgage of property: mortgages over real estate must be executed before a public notary (or equivalent official) and registered with the Land Registry Office (*Conservatória do Registo Predial*) to be valid. If agreed by the parties, the mortgagee can be a beneficiary of the proceeds of insurance entered into to cover the risks of the mortgaged property. A mortgagee does not have the right to take possession of a property in the event of a default in payment of the secured obligation, but only the right to a judicial sale of the property and to be paid the proceeds of such a sale. The normal procedure is the enforcement of the security by means of seizure, that is, by the judicial apprehension of the asset provided as a guarantee and conferring on the creditor the right to be paid out of the proceeds of the sale of the assets, with priority over other creditors provided there is no prior security in rem over the attached assets. In a judicial sale, the property is sold free of any charges and encumbrances.

(ii) Assignment of revenues (*consignação de rendimentos*): the assignment of revenues secures the fulfilment of an obligation to the creditor, who is entitled to be paid from the revenues of any relevant asset (e.g., real estate, shares). The granting of this security requires a deed, which in the case of real estate, cannot exceed fifteen years in duration and must be registered in the Land Registry Office. In other cases, the assignment of revenues may last for a fixed number of years or until the secured obligation has been satisfied.

(iii) Pledge of *quotas* or shares: in the case of a limited liability company by shares, a pledge of shares has to be recorded in the company's share registry book, as well as on the certificates or in the relevant security account if the shares are book-entry. In limited liability companies by *quotas*, the pledge of the shares must be registered with the Commercial Registry Office. Without prejudice to the above, all pledges take effect once the company is informed in writing or expressly or tacitly acknowledges them.

(iv) Book debt/receivables/insurances: a pledge or an assignment by way of security can be granted over receivables, which in both cases must be notified to the debtor. An assignment by way of security can be granted over future receivables if they can be determined. For example, Portuguese law allows assignments by way of security of rents arising from real estate leases.

(v) Pledge of bank accounts: the preferred method is a financial pledge over the balance of specified bank accounts. The bank must be notified of the pledge but is not required to give its consent.

(vi) Intellectual property: intellectual property rights can be pledged, and the pledge must be registered with the IP Institute (*Instituto Nacional da Propriedade Industrial*).

[139] Without prejudice to the above, attention must always be paid to the articles of association of the relevant companies, as these may contain, for instance, additional requirements for the creation of guarantees, such as shareholders' consent.

[140] As regards creditors, the rules of priority ranking are generally as follows:

(i) remuneration of employees;

(ii) judicial expenses incurred directly for the common interest of the creditors for the preservation, execution or liquidation of real estate properties;

(iii) amounts due to the tax authorities;
(iv) social security payments;
(v) any credit secured by retention right (*direito de retenção*); and
(vi) mortgage payments in compliance with the priority arising from the relevant registry.

[141] Without prejudice to the above, in an insolvency scenario, specific rules set out in the general framework established for insolvency proceedings will apply.

[142] The timing of the process for enforcement of security varies. For example, enforcement proceedings in relation to mortgages take, on average, a period of between one and three years when there is no appeal.

[143] The enforcement of security is the main remedy. If there are mortgages and other real security, the lenders have preference over other creditors, provided that there is no prior security in rem over the secured assets.

[144] Securitisation is not very common in real estate finance, but sale and lease-back are very frequent.

2.6.4 Purchase of Own Shares

[145] Subscription by a company for its own shares is forbidden, and the purchase by a company of its own shares has several limits. As long as the shares belong to the company, the following rules apply:

(i) all rights inherent to the shares are regarded as suspended, except for the right of the holder to receive new shares in the case of a capital increase by capitalisation of reserves;
(ii) a reserve equal to the amount for which they are accounted becomes unavailable;
(iii) in the annual report of the Board of Directors or of the Executive Board of Directors, the following must be clearly indicated:
  (a) the number of own shares acquired during the financial year, the reasons for the acquisitions made and the expenses incurred by the company in acquiring them; and
  (b) the number of own shares sold during the financial year, the reasons for the disposals made and the expenses incurred by the company in disposing of them.
  (c) the number of the company's own shares held by the company at the end of the financial year.

[146] A company that has limited liability by *quotas* may not acquire its own *quotas* that have not been fully paid, except where the amount of a quota is lost in the case of exclusion of a partner. Own *quotas* may only be acquired by the company free of charge, or in an executive action brought against the partner, or if, for this purpose, the company has free reserves in an amount not less than twice the amount to be paid.

[147] In the case of a company of limited liability by shares, the articles of association may prohibit the acquisition of its own shares in its entirety or reduce the cases in which it is permitted by law. Also, the company may not acquire and hold its own shares representing more than 10% of its capital, except when:

(i) the acquisition aims at satisfying provisions of the law by the company;
(ii) the acquisition is intended to implement a capital reduction resolution;
(iii) the acquisition is a result of a universal transfer of the company's assets;
(iv) the acquisition is made free of charge;
(v) the acquisition is made in an enforcement procedure for the recovery of third-party debts or by a transaction in a declaratory action proposed for the same purpose; and
(vi) the acquisition is made through a procedure established by law or in the articles of association for the non-release of shares by its subscribers.

[148] The company may not hold shares in excess of the 10% limit for a period of more than three years, even if they were lawfully acquired.

[149] In exchange for the acquisition of its own shares, a company may only deliver assets which are distributable to shareholders, and the value of the distributable assets must be at least equal to twice the value payable for them.

[150] Shares illegally acquired by the company must be sold within the year following their acquisition (i.e., in cases where the law does not render their acquisition null and void). Failure to do so will result in the cancellation of the relevant shares. Additionally, the directors will become liable, in general terms, for damages suffered by the company, its creditors or third parties as a result of the illegal acquisition of shares, the cancellation of shares or the lack of cancellation of shares.

2.6.5 Completion Formalities

[151] The completion formalities are mainly influenced by (i) the type of company; (ii) the sector; (iii) the type of assets acquired; and (iv) the type of the deal.

[152] While the assignment of *quotas* is subject to registration with the Commercial Registry Office, the transfer of shares involves the updating of the share register book and the endorsement of the share certificates in the case of registered shares; and the transfer of book-entry securities between accounts, in the case of book-entry shares.

[153] Furthermore, communications and other formalities may be required in relation to relevant regulators when applicable.

[154] Moreover, transactions which include any type of real estate (real property, rural, agricultural or urban land) may be subject to additional formalities.

[155] Title to real estate is evidenced by a land registry certificate (*certidão predial*) issued by the Land Registry Office. Additionally, under Portuguese law, all real estate must have a property tax registry certificate (*caderneta predial*) issued by the Portuguese Tax Authority (*Autoridade Tributária*) (AT).

[156] The land registry certificate is a public record of each property's legal status, including ownership and encumbrances. The land registry certificate contains:

(i) a specific description of the plot or building, including area measurements and type of property (that is, urban or rural); and
(ii) registered rights or restrictions on the property, including any acquisitions, liens, mortgages or encumbrances.

[157] The tax registry certificate certifies the registration of the property with the AT.

[158] As soon as it is clear that the property meets or is capable of meeting the requirements of the buyer, a promissory purchase and sale agreement (*contrato promessa de compra e venda*) may be executed between the seller and the buyer. This agreement is binding and must include all the conditions precedent that need to be fulfilled before the purchase and sale can be completed.

[159] A sale and purchase agreement (*contrato de compra e venda*), executed through a private agreement (certified by a lawyer or a paralegal officer) or a notarial deed, can be concluded at the end of an agreed period of time allowed for fulfilment of the conditions precedent which were included in the promissory agreement.

[160] The promissory purchase and sale agreement must be signed by the parties, and in order for the agreement to be directly enforceable in court, the signatures of the buyer and the seller must be certified by a notary or lawyer with reference to the use permit/building permit (as applicable).

[161] It is usual to provide an advance payment (*sinal*). By law, as a general rule, in case of default by the promissory purchaser, the promissory seller is entitled to retain the down payment received. In the case of default by the promissory seller, the promissory purchaser is entitled to receive an amount equal to twice the down payment. Alternatively, specific performance (*execução específica*) of the promissory agreement may be sought by the non-defaulting party, allowing either party to request that the court should enforce the contract instead of paying a penalty or compensation.

[162] Mortgages are registered in the Land Registry Office, and buyers are advised to make a thorough investigation to ensure that no charges or encumbrances (such as rights of way) exist, even where none are shown on the register.

[163] It is also important to check for the existence of any pre-emption rights, such as rights in favour of the relevant municipality, the Portuguese State (through the National Department for Cultural Heritage – *Direção-Geral do Património Cultural*), tenants and neighbours of rural properties.

[164] The promissory sale agreement will already have contained representations and warranties (R&Ws) by the parties, and these are usually repeated in the notarial deed.

[165] A 'time to remedy is usually granted, and where no remedy is possible, an indemnity is paid by the seller to the buyer. Such an indemnity is usually secured by a bank guarantee, a bond or an escrow account. As regards the duration of R&Ws,

a general term of around eighteen months would be market standard, except for those R&Ws related to title, capacity, charges, labour, social security and tax, all of which would be subject to the applicable legal statute of limitation.

[166] Where the defects are disclosed to and accepted by the buyer before the sale is concluded, the seller's liability can be limited to the extent of the defects disclosed.

[167] The seller is liable for non-disclosure of information about material defects in the property.

[168] The property is transferred by notarial deed or by a certified private document, in which case, it may be executed before a lawyer or a paralegal officer. The main documents required for the completion of the sale are:

(i) land registry certificate (*certidão predial*);
(ii) tax certificate (*caderneta predial*);
(iii) use permit (*licença de utilização*);
(iv) energy certificate (*certificado energético*);
(v) technical file (*ficha técnica*), if applicable;
(vi) evidence that public entities have not decided to exercise their pre-emption right to acquire the property (if applicable);
(vii) declaration from the condominium manager, with the amount of all condominium charges in force in relation to the unit, specifying their nature, respective amounts, payment deadlines, and, if any, the existing debts related to the building unit to be sold, specifying the respective nature, amounts, constitution and due dates.
(viii) proof of payment or of exemption from Property Transfer Tax (*Imposto Municipal sobre as Transmissões Onerosas de Imóveis*) (IMT) and Stamp Duty (*Imposto do Selo*).

[169] Recently, proof of registration of the ultimate beneficial owner with the Portuguese Ministry of Justice is also required by law for corporate entities, as well as evidence of the bank transfer or of the bank cheque used for the payment of the consideration.

[170] The acquisition of properties must be registered with the Land Registry Office and the tax authorities. Registration is evidence of ownership of the relevant property. The promissory agreement applies from its signing until execution of the notarial deed.

2.6.6 Costs and Fees

[171] In M&A transactions, in addition to costs and expenses arising from the parties' own teams and professional advisers, tax costs are very often the most relevant, particularly when the transfer of immovable property is involved.

[172] The acquisition of real estate within the Portuguese tax jurisdiction is, in general, subject to IMT at a rate of 6.5% on urban property or land for construction and 5% on rural property. Within the category of urban property, residential property is subject to special progressive rates between 0% and 7.5%, depending on the value of the property. Stamp duty also falls upon transfers of real estate at a flat rate of 0.8% and, like IMT, is payable by the buyer. The applicable stamp duty and IMT rates are due either on the purchase price of the transaction or on the tax registration value (*valor patrimonial tributário*, normally referred to as VPT), whichever is higher.

[173] The acquisition of property for resale within three years is exempt from IMT, provided certain requirements are met.

[174] Other tax exemption regimes are available for the acquisition of:

(i) property acquired for urban rehabilitation;
(ii) buildings individually classified as national monuments and buildings subject to public or municipal interest;
(iii) real estate by companies when the assets are considered as investments eligible for specific EU-approved incentives, following specific authorisations by municipalities.

[175] M&A transactions may be exempted from IMT and Stamp Duty whenever they fit into the categories laid down in the Tax Incentives Code (*Estatuto dos Benefícios Fiscais*), and their positive effect on the economy can be demonstrated by an *ad hoc* economic study carried out by the companies involved and which is properly documented and made available to the AT. Any reorganisations having as their sole or primary aim a tax advantage will not be exempt from the aforesaid taxes and may be subject to penalty interest at the rate of 15% on the amount of tax wrongfully withheld by the companies concerned.

[176] It should also be noted that the acquisition of *quotas* and shares in respect of a limited liability company by *quotas* or by shares is subject to property transfer tax at the rates referred to above when cumulatively: (i) the value of the company's assets derives, directly or indirectly, in more than 50% from immovable property situated in the national territory, considering the balance sheet value or, if higher, the VPT; (ii) such real estate is not directly allocated to an agricultural, industrial or commercial activity, excluding the purchase and sale of real estate; and (iii) that acquisition, amortisation or any other facts result in the acquirer owning, after the acquisition, at least 75% of the share capital of the company in question.

[177] The transfer of a business as a *going concern* involved in an M&A transaction is excluded from VAT but may be subject to Stamp Duty at a rate of 5% wherever the transfer of such a business entails goodwill and transfer of the position of lessor of the establishment where the business activity is undertaken.

[178] M&A transactions are subject to several disclosure requirements and ancillary obligations whenever they benefit from the special neutrality regime (i.e., the transposition into Portuguese law of the EU Merger Directive provisions). Apart from the obligation to report in the annual tax declaration, the participation in a tax-neutral operation (an obligation which, in principle, falls upon the receiving company), the companies involved must issue certain statements or obtain proof that they fulfil all the subjective and objective conditions required to benefit from the special neutrality regime.

[179] It is also noteworthy that, in general, EUR250.00 is payable for each property transfer registration in the Land Registry Office. All buildings must have an energy certificate (*certificado de energético*). Some exceptions to this are buildings or autonomous units of buildings used as warehouses, workshops or parking areas. The certificate is evidence of compliance with legal requirements concerning energy efficiency and air quality inside the buildings. A penalty of between EUR250.00 and EUR3 740.00 (for individuals) and between EUR2 500.00 and EUR44 890.00 (for companies) may apply, particularly if the owner sells the property without delivering the energy certificate to the buyer.

2.6.7 Insolvency

[180] Under Portuguese law, the buying of shares and businesses of companies which have gone into insolvency can be contemplated under different structures. These options need to be accessed on a case-by-case basis, taking into account notably the nature, activity and business of the company, its creditors, the assets included in the insolvency estate (*massa insolvente*) and the applicable legal requirements under insolvency proceedings. It should be noted that, as a general rule, by entering into insolvency proceedings, the insolvent entity is subject to restrictions in relation to the management and disposal of its assets. In this regard, the declaration of insolvency deprives the insolvent entity – either by itself or through its directors – of the powers to manage and sell assets under the insolvency estate, which powers are assigned to the insolvency administrator. Therefore, any purchase of shares and businesses must take into account the specific substantive and procedural requirements envisaged for this type of transaction.

[181] Disregarding certain special procedures existing under Portuguese law (such as the Special Revitalization Procedure (*Processo Especial de Revitalização*)), common market practice and the Portuguese insolvency legal framework would normally dictate that such an acquisition may be carried out in four different ways: (i) the conversion of credits into share capital; (ii) restructuring by transfer of the company; (iii) the extra-judicial acquisition of shares; and (iv) the acquisition of the company by means of the liquidation of its insolvent assets.

[182] However, these transactions do not exhaust all the possibilities envisaged by law. In this regard, it is possible to establish an insolvency plan (*plano de insolvência*) for the company, approving measures beyond the straightforward liquidation and payment of the company's creditors – notably the assignment of assets to the creditors, amendments to the company's by-laws, or the company's transformation into a different type of company. The law does not envisage a strict set of measures to be included under such a plan, and therefore, the parties may combine or agree upon different measures.[3]

[3] Without prejudice to the existence of certain limitations, such as principle of equality between creditors.

[183] Furthermore, the proposal of an insolvency plan may be submitted by a creditor or group of creditors whose credits represent at least one-fifth of the total of the non-subordinated credits as per the ranking and validation decision issued by the court (and should be subject to approval by the creditors and by the court). Hence, any entity intending to purchase companies subject to insolvency procedures should carefully assess the measures and effectiveness of the insolvency plan.

[184] It is recommended that the purchase of insolvent companies should be accompanied by normal due diligence procedures prior to the acquisition. Apart from complying with the procedural and substantive requirements applicable within insolvency procedures, further consideration should be given to the existence of all elements required for the company to proceed with its business or activity, in particular, administrative licences and permits, material contracts, insurance, and other rights such as intellectual property rights, or any potential regulatory requirements, such as authorisation from the competition authorities.

[185] We outline below a high-level overview of the transactions referred to above for the purposes of buying shares or businesses which have gone into insolvency. This does not entail all applicable requirements or provide an exhaustive description of all the risks involved. As noted, the nature and risks of each transaction must be assessed on a case-by-case basis.

Conversion of Credits into Share Capital

[186] The conversion of credits into share capital (debt to equity swap) is one of the measures which may be approved under an insolvency plan and which allow the company's creditors to become shareholders or to further increase the number of their shares. Under this type of transaction, the creditor will not be entitled to payment but only to the conversion of the credits into share capital. As a general rule, such conversion is subject to the prior consent of the creditor whose credits are subject to conversion. Nevertheless, the law envisages the possibility of converting credits to share capital without prior consent of the relevant creditor if certain conditions are met (e.g., the company's by-laws do not envisage any restrictions on the assignment of shares).[4]

[187] This transaction will favour the company's balance sheet, bearing in mind that the debts corresponding to such credits will be written off due to the conversion to share capital. As noted above, the execution of this transaction may be combined with other types of measures, such as changes to the company's by-laws or the appointment of new members to the board of directors.

The Restructuring by Transfer of the Company

[188] The restructuring by transfer of the company allows for the acquisition of the business through the purchase of its assets. This type of transaction corresponds to

[4] It should be noted that prior to insolvency, further consideration may be given to the possibility of proceeding with the conversion of credits into share capital, as a measure directed at preventing the beginning of insolvency procedures, under the Legal Framework of Conversion of Credits into Share Capital (*Regime jurídico da conversão de créditos em capital*) approved by Law No. 7/2018, of 2 March.

an asset deal (*trespasse*), under which the insolvency plan envisages the incorporation of one or more companies destined to operate one or more establishments purchased from the insolvency estate in exchange for appropriate consideration. Moreover, the by-laws of such companies should be attached to the insolvency plan.

[189] The transfer of the company should also be considered in light of the effects of such a transaction on certain agreements, such as employment and lease agreements and the requirements of the applicable legislation. In particular, such a transaction is also likely to result in the transfer of employment contracts to the buyer.

The Extra-Judicial Acquisition of Shares

[190] Portuguese law does not expressly envisage the possibility of purchasing shares of insolvent companies. This type of transaction was previously prohibited under the prior insolvency regime, but this prohibition was subsequently revoked by the PIC.

[191] Even though this may be debatable, it seems that it may be possible to execute a transaction of this nature. Nevertheless, there is a risk that the buyer ultimately ends up purchasing shares of a company which is subject to extinction due to the termination of the insolvency procedure. Thus, the buyer should carefully weigh up the risks of entering into a transaction of this nature – in particular, by liaising with the relevant parties – in order to prevent the negative consequences arising (in particular) from the termination of the insolvency proceedings or from the expectations of an approved insolvency plan being frustrated. Moreover, the buyer should weigh up the likelihood of the company's creditors ultimately approving an insolvency plan which envisages the continuation of the company's business.

The Acquisition of the Company Through the Liquidation of the Insolvent Assets

[192] As a general rule, an insolvency administrator should proceed with the sale of the company as a whole unless there is no satisfactory offer of consideration or unless there is some perceived advantage in the separate liquidation or sale of certain parts of the company. This transaction is similar to the restructuring by transfer of the company as referred to above.

[193] Since this type of transaction is deemed an act of special importance (*ato de especial relevo*), the insolvency administrator should obtain prior authorisation from the commission of creditors or, if this body does not exist, from the creditors' assembly. Therefore, it is advisable for the buyer to confirm that all necessary authorisations have been granted prior to executing the transaction. Moreover, the approval of an insolvency plan may provide for specific measures involving the company's assets, including in relation to those assets eventually subject to separate liquidation or sale under Article 162(1) of the PIC.

[194] Finally, as noted above in relation to the restructuring by transfer of the company, the acquisition of the company through the liquidation of the insolvent assets must also be assessed in the light of the existence of certain agreements, such as employment and lease agreements and the requirements envisaged under applicable legislation.

2.6.8 Choice of Law

[195] Without prejudice to EU regulations on these matters, according to the Portuguese Civil Procedure Code (*Código de Processo Civil*) (PCPC), the parties may agree upon which jurisdiction will be competent to settle a specific dispute, or any disputes arising from a particular legal relationship, so long as that relationship is connected with more than one legal system.

[196] The legal requirements for a jurisdiction agreement to be enforceable in Portugal are set out in the PCPC and are as follows:

(i) the dispute in question must be related to alienable rights (meaning those which can be freely disposed of by their holder – for example, the right to life is an inalienable right);
(ii) it (i.e., the jurisdiction agreement) is accepted by the law of the chosen forum;
(iii) it is justified by a material interest of both parties or of one of the parties provided that it does not involve a serious inconvenience for the other;
(iv) it does not involve a matter falling exclusively to the jurisdiction of the Portuguese courts; and
(v) it is made or confirmed in writing containing an express reference to the competent jurisdiction.

[197] It is open to the parties to conclude an arbitration agreement whereby they undertake to submit a specific dispute, or any dispute arising from a certain legal relationship, to arbitration.

[198] The legal requirements for an arbitration agreement to be enforceable in Portugal are set out in the Portuguese Arbitration Law (*Lei de Arbitragem Voluntária*) (PAL).

[199] Pursuant to those provisions, the arbitration agreement may refer to an existing dispute (submission agreement), in which case the agreement should determine the subject matter of the dispute, or it may refer to any future disputes arising from a specific legal relationship of a contractual or extra-contractual nature (arbitration clause).

[200] Pursuant to PAL, the arbitration agreement must be concluded in writing. The law further provides that this requirement is fulfilled if it is recorded on an electronic, magnetic, optical or any other type of basis offering the same guarantees of reliability, comprehensiveness and preservation.

[201] In the case of international arbitration, PAL provides that the arbitration agreement will be regarded as valid if it meets the requirements of either the law chosen by the parties to govern the arbitration agreement, the law applicable to the subject matter of the dispute, or Portuguese law.

2.7 Specific Rules on Public Takeovers

2.7.1 Public Offers

[202] M&A transactions aiming at obtaining control over a company with shares admitted to trading on a regulated market located in Portugal (e.g., Euronext Lisbon) are specially regulated by provisions set out in the Portuguese Securities Code, as well as in regulations issued by CMVM. Those rules define the structure, content and procedure for formalising a takeover bid (*oferta pública de aquisição* – OPA).

[203] Takeover bids may be of a voluntary or mandatory nature. A takeover bid will be mandatory (subject to certain exceptions) where a shareholder acquires, directly or indirectly, more than one-third or 50% of the voting rights corresponding to the share capital. The takeover bid will not be mandatory where the shareholder proves to the CMVM that it cannot exercise a dominant influence over the target (in which case the shareholder will be required to disclose to the CMVM anytime its shareholding in the target is increased by over 1%).

[204] While voluntary bids may be only partial, mandatory takeover bids must include all shares (and other securities which may confer share subscription or acquisition rights) of the target.

[205] For takeover bids, the particular formalities required, such as approvals and acceptances, are the main hurdles to be considered, as well as the many deadlines within which such authorisations must be achieved. The main consents required are the resolutions of the competent board or person launching the bid, authorisation by the CMVM and, in some cases, other mandatory consents by regulated authorities.

[206] The offeror, the target company, its shareholders and the members of corporate bodies, as well as all those who render services to them on a permanent or occasional basis, must keep the preparation of the bid secret until the preliminary announcement has been published. The offeror must submit a preliminary announcement to the CMVM, to the target company and to the relevant stock exchange managing entities in which the target company is listed. The preliminary announcement must include, among other things, the following information:

- (i) the identification of the offeror and of the target company;
- (ii) the identification of the securities subject to the offer;
- (iii) the consideration payable in respect of the offer;
- (iv) the financial intermediary in charge of assisting the bid (if appointed);
- (v) the percentage of voting rights of the target company held by the offeror (in accordance with the applicable voting rights imputation rules);
- (vi) a summary of the offeror's intentions regarding, notably, the continuity or alteration of the business activity of the target company, of the offeror and of their controlling or controlled entities;
- (vii) the offeror's status regarding the limitation of the target's powers and potential suspension of restrictions on voting and share transfers;

(viii) in case the offeror is under a duty to proceed with a takeover bid, the offeror's intention to ask for its dismissal under the exception to such duty legally established for the cases where the thresholds for the mandatory bid have been met as a result of a takeover bid over the totality of the target's shares in the terms required by law; and
(ix) the conditions or legal assumptions to which the offer is subject.

[207] [The publication of the preliminary announcement requires the offeror to (i) launch the bid on terms no less favourable to the addressees than those set out in that preliminary announcement; (ii) request the registration of the bid within twenty days, extendable by the CMVM up to sixty days in exchange public offers; and (iii) to inform the representatives of its employees or (in the absence of any such representatives) the employees themselves, of the contents of the offer documents, as soon as they are made public.

[208] The prospectus must include information on:

(i) the identification of the offeror and the issuer;
(ii) the identification, characteristics and amount of securities subject to the offer;
(iii) the type of offer;
(iv) the consideration offered, its justification and the conditions for payment both in national market as well as in foreign market (if applicable);
(v) the minimum and maximum amount of securities the offeror proposes to acquire
(vi) the offer period;
(vii) the allotment criteria;
(viii) the conditions precedent to the offer;
(ix) the entity responsible for the counting and disclosure of the offer results;
(x) the percentage of voting rights held by the offeror in the target, and vice versa (in accordance with the applicable voting rights imputation rules);
(xi) securities of the same category as those subject to the bid which have been acquired, or undertaken to do so, in the previous six months by the offeror or related entities (with indication of the relevant acquisition dates, quantities and consideration);
(xii) the offeror's intentions regarding, notably, *(i)* the continuity or alteration of the business activity of the target company, of the offeror and of their controlling or controlled entities, *(ii)* the labour conditions of the respective employees and directors and *(iii)* maintenance, or not, of the listing of the securities which are the object of the offer on a regulated market;
(xiii) the financing of the bid and the possible implications of the bid's completion on the offeror's financial position;
(xiv) any shareholder agreements entered into by the offeror or by related entities which may have a significant impact on the target company;
(xv) any agreements made between the offeror or related entities and the members of the target's governing bodies, including any special benefits established in their favour;

(xvi) the compensation offered and the conditions for payment in case of suppression of voting or share transfer rights under the applicable rules;
(xvii) the competent courts and the law applicable to contracts concluded between the offeror and the holders of securities of the target company following acceptance of the bid; and
(xviii) any charges to be borne by the addressees of the bid.

[209] If unforeseen and material changes in the circumstances occur, CMVM is empowered to authorise the offeror to modify or revoke the offer. In any case, CMVM may authorise the offeror to review its offer's terms and conditions until two days before the term of the offer, provided that any changes do not render it less favourable as a whole to the addressees.

2.7.2 Stakebuilding

[210] In principle, stakebuilding prior to the preliminary announcement, i.e., in the preparatory phase of the offer, may raise market abuse concerns and should be viewed with caution.

[211] From the publication of the preliminary announcement and up to the date on which the result of the offer is calculated, the offeror, as well as related individuals or entities:

(i) must not negotiate, outside a regulated market, for the acquisition or sale of any securities of the same category as those comprising the offer or the consideration for the offer, except if authorised by the CMVM; and
(ii) must inform the CMVM on a daily basis regarding transactions carried out relating to the securities issued by the target company or to the category of securities comprised in the consideration.

2.7.3 Break Fees

[212] The agreement by a target company of break fees with a bidder may be considered an unlawful benefit to the bidder, but this is a highly contentious issue in the Portuguese legal world.

2.7.4 Price

[213] The consideration in takeover bids may consist of (i) cash; (ii) securities issued or to be issued, or (iii) may be mixed. If the consideration consists of cash, the offeror must, prior to registration of the bid, deposit the full amount with a credit institution or present an appropriate bank guarantee. If the consideration consists of securities, these must have adequate liquidity and be easy to appraise.

[214] Any acquisition of securities of the category which are the subject of the offer, or of those which are part of the consideration, made after the publication of the preliminary announcement, must be included in the calculation of the minimum quantity which the offeror proposes to acquire and if such transactions occur, the offeror is required to increase the consideration to a price not lower than the highest price paid for the securities so acquired.

2.7.5 Duties of the Target Company and Its Board of Directors

[215] Buyers may rely on the availability of certain public information as Portuguese companies must make numerous filings at the competent commercial registry offices. Furthermore, certain companies and issuers of securities admitted to trading on a regulated market are subject to disclosure duties under which they must make available different information, such as (i) the articles of association; (ii) annual, half-yearly and quarterly (if applicable) financial statements and management reports; (iii) appointments of directors and of statutory auditors; and (iv) privileged information.

[216] The launch of a takeover bid results in an obligation on the board of the target company to prepare a report (to be published) containing specific information regarding the terms, conditions and potential impacts of the proposed bid, and in which it can give its opinion, whether in favour of or against the bid. The report shall be issued within eight days, counting from the date of reception of the prospectus draft (or five days counting from receipt of any revised versions as determined by the CMVM or the publication of any addenda to the prospectus). Normally, the tone of the report will determine whether the submitted bid may be considered hostile or friendly, and in this way, a negative or positive opinion can materially influence the outcome of the bid.

[217] As the board of directors of the target company is subject to a duty of 'passivity' or neutrality, it is not possible in principle for the board to assist a preferred bidder to succeed with the transaction or to frustrate the intervention by a competitor, as such actions may be considered a breach of the board's fiduciary duties and of the principle of neutrality and/or passivity. Any steps taken by the board in this regard may be deemed unlawful. However, the board may approve and recommend the deal to its shareholders and may agree not to take frustrating action (a negative commitment).

[218] In fact, the duty of passivity imposed on the board of directors of the target company may give some comfort to the bidder, as the bidder generally has no control over the target company during the entire bid process (except perhaps in voluntary bids, where it may be possible to gain some control over the target company by making the bid conditional on specified events, always provided that such conditions are aligned with the bidder's interests and do not affect the normal functioning of the market). Mandatory takeovers cannot be subject to any conditions other than those related to regulatory approvals.

2.7.6 Types of Takeovers

Friendly and Hostile Takeovers

[219] There is no legal concept of a hostile takeover in the PSC, and Portuguese law makes no distinction between a friendly or hostile acquisition or takeover. However, it is quite common for such a distinction to be made in the context of the response to the bid by the target company's board of directors and/or by the relevant shareholders.

[220] Furthermore, hostile bids are not only allowed but are relatively common. In fact, the public takeover offers announced by Sonae for Portugal Telecom and by Banco Comercial Português, S.A. (presently called MillenniumBcp) for Banco BPI, S.A., which were the two most significant public takeovers announced in recent years, were both hostile.

Mandatory Takeovers

[221] The duty to launch a mandatory takeover bid is imposed on any shareholder whose shareholding, directly or indirectly, exceeds the thresholds of one-third and 50%, respectively of the voting rights, provided that the excess does not result from one of the following: (i) an acquisition of securities occurring as a result of a takeover offer launched for all the securities issued by the target company, without any restriction as to the maximum quantity or percentage of securities to be acquired; (ii) the implementation of a financial recovery plan within the framework of one of the methods of recovery or reorganisation provided for by law, including the implementation of resolution measures or the exercise of powers to terminate or reduce or convert own funds instruments to credit institutions or financial companies in accordance with the law; (iii) merger of companies, if the resolution of the general meeting of shareholders issuing the securities in respect of which the offer would be addressed expressly states that the operation would result in the duty to launch a takeover bid; (iv) an acquisition of securities through inheritance, as long as the company's articles of association provide for such transfer.

[222] Additionally, the launch of a mandatory bid is not required if, after exceeding the limit of one-third or 50%, the acquiring entity proves to CMVM that, in practice, it cannot exercise a dominant influence over the target company.

[223] The duty to launch a takeover bid may be suspended if the obliged entity, in a written communication addressed to the CMVM immediately after the event imposing the duty to launch the bid, undertakes to put an end to the situation within the following 120 days. During the period of suspension of the duty to launch the bid, the acquirer's voting rights are inhibited to the extent that they exceed the relevant limit.

[224] The consideration for a mandatory bid may not be less than the higher of the following amounts:

(i) the highest price paid or undertaken to be paid by the offeror, or by any of his related persons, for the acquisition of securities of the same class in the six months immediately preceding the date of publication of the preliminary offer notice; and

(ii) the weighted average price of those securities on a regulated market over the same period.

[225] In cases where the consideration cannot be determined by reference to these criteria above or where the CMVM considers that the consideration, in cash or in securities, proposed by the offeror is not duly justified or is not equitable (being either insufficient or excessive), the minimum consideration may be set at the offeror's expense by an independent auditor appointed by the CMVM. If the value determined by the independent auditor is lower than the value determined according to (i) above, the latter will prevail. Conversely, if the value determined by the independent auditor is lower than the value determined according to (ii) above, such lower value determined by the independent auditor prevails.

2.7.7 Offer Period

[226] The offer period may vary between two and ten weeks, and CMVM has the power to extend the bid period in the event of any revision of bid terms, the launch of a competing bid, or when the protection of the interests of the addressees so justifies, whether on its own initiative or at the request of the offeror.

2.7.8 Squeeze-Out and Sell-Out Rights

[227] If following the launch of a takeover bid, the offeror reaches or exceeds, whether directly or indirectly, 90% of the voting rights attributable to the existing share capital (prior to the results of the bid being ascertained), may within the following three months acquire the remaining shares for a consideration in cash.

[228] Each remaining minority shareholder continuing in such circumstances to hold shares may, within three months from the result of the bid, exercise a right of disposal and, to this end, must address a written invitation to the controlling shareholder to make a proposal for the acquisition of his shares within eight days.

[229] In the absence of any such proposal by the controlling shareholder or if such proposal is not considered satisfactory, any holder of remaining shares may make a proposal for such disposal by means of a declaration addressed to the CMVM and accompanied by specific documentation.

[230] Once the requirement for disposal has been verified by the CMVM, the disposal becomes effective upon notification by CMVM to the controlling shareholder, and the certificate attesting to the notification constitutes an enforcement order.

2.7.9 Administrative Offences

[231] In this context, the breach of a number of these duties is regarded as an administrative offence and is subject to the application of fines, which range between:

(i) EUR25 000 and EUR5 000 000 for very serious offences;
(ii) EUR12 500 and EUR2 500 000 for serious offences; and
(iii) EUR5 000 and EUR1 000 000 for minor offences.

[232] The higher range amounts can be increased in certain cases, and ancillary sanctions may also apply.

[233] Undertaking a public offer without the approval of the prospectus or its registration with the CMVM is an example of a very serious offence.

[234] Similarly, the breach of, *inter alia*, the following duties would constitute very serious offences:

(i) equality of treatment and allotment rules;
(ii) disclosure of the offer documents, addenda and final conditions;
(iii) duty of secrecy relating to the preparation of public bids;
(iv) publication of the preliminary takeover bid preliminary announcement;
(v) application for takeover bid registration as well as the launch of a bid following the publication of the preliminary announcement;
(vi) launching of mandatory takeover bids;
(vii) duties relating to transactions during the offer/stakebuilding; and
(viii) duty to increase the consideration to a price that is not lower than the highest price paid for securities acquired in transactions carried out pending mandatory takeover bids.

[235] In general terms, the application of fines by the CMVM is subject to judicial appeal.

2.8 Other Relevant Laws and Due Diligence Issues

2.8.1 Anti-bribery/Anti-corruption/AML

[236] There are no anti-bribery or anti-corruption laws directly or specifically affecting M&A activity in Portugal and the US Foreign Corrupt Practices Act (FCPA) does not seem to have had any direct effect in practice on M&A activity in Portugal.

[237] However, in December 2021, two laws implementing the National Anti-Corruption Strategy 2020–2024 were published, namely Decree-Law 109-E/2021 of December 9 ('General Regime of Prevention of Corruption') and Law 93/2021 of December 20 ('General Regime of Protection of Whistleblowers'), which have already come into force. The entry into force of these laws brings new obligations for entities with more than fifty employees, making it mandatory to adopt and implement a regulatory compliance program with corruption prevention measures, as well as a whistleblowing channel that must include reports on any corruption conducts.

[238] Moreover, the following Portuguese legislation recognises some basic offences in the areas of bribery and corruption:

(i) Portuguese Criminal Code (*Código Penal*), enacted by Decree-Law No. 400/82, 23 September:
  (a) undue receipt (or offering) of an advantage by (or to) a public official;
  (b) passive and active corruption in the public sector, punishable under Articles 373 and 374 of the Portuguese Criminal Code (Decree-Law No. 400/82, 23 September);
(ii) Law on Crimes of the Responsibility of Political Officials (*Crimes da Responsabilidade de Titulares de Cargos Políticos*), enacted by Law No. 34/87, 16 July:
  (a) undue receipt of an advantage by a political or high public official;
  (b) passive and active corruption of political and high public officials;
(iii) Law on active corruption in international commerce and passive and active corruption in the private sector, enacted by Law No. 20/2008, 21 April;
(iv) Military Justice Code (*Código de Justiça Militar*), enacted by Law No. 100/2003, 15 November:
  (a) passive corruption of an individual serving in the Armed Forces or other military forces;
  (b) active corruption of an individual serving in the Armed Forces or other military forces;
(v) Criminal Regime for Unsporting Behaviors (*Regime de Responsabilidade Penal por Comportamentos Antidesportivos)*, enacted by Law No. 50/2007, 31 August:
  (a) passive and active corruption of a sports agent;
  (b) undue receipt (or offering) of an advantage by (or to) a sports agent.

[239] According to the *Corruption Perception Index*, published by the *Transparency International* organisation, Portugal's ranking has been stable for the last decade (30th among 180 countries).[5]

[240] During the last decade, we have seen a significant number of corruption cases being prosecuted by the judicial authorities, some of which have involved high-profile individuals in both the political and economic sectors. We believe that this is not a sign of any increase in corruption in Portugal but rather an indication that the Portuguese political and judicial authorities have taken a step forward in the fight against corruption.

[241] Law No. 83/2017, 18 August, which transposed the Directives No. 2015/849/EU of the European Parliament and of the Council of 20 May 2015 and No. 2016/2258/EU of the Council of 6 December 2016, sets out a vast number of regulatory duties to its *obliged entities* (financial entities and certain non-financial entities) which are aimed to fight and prevent money laundering and terrorist financing activities.

2.8.2 Environmental/Product Safety

[242] In Portugal, both public and private projects that are likely to have negative effects on the environment are subject to environmental impact assessment. This assessment aims to identify and quantify the environmental effects of these projects

[5] https://transparencia.pt/cpi2019/.

and to identify measures to avoid, minimise or offset these effects, as well as methods for monitoring their progress.

[243] The legal framework is provided by Decree-Law No. 151-B/2013 of 31 October, as amended by Decree-Law No. 152-B/2017, which transposed into Portuguese law the corresponding EU Directives.

[244] The projects subject to this procedure are identified in the legislation referred to above, and a decision regarding the environmental impact assessment is necessarily made prior to the licensing or authorisation of those projects. The decision is taken by the competent authority, which generally corresponds to the Environmental Impact Assessment Authority (*Agência Portuguesa do Ambiente*) ('EIA Authority').

[245] The subject entities should submit an environmental impact assessment study, accompanied by the prior study, preliminary project, or the execution project in question, which will be assessed and posted for public consultation.

[246] The decision regarding the environmental impact statement (*declaração de impacte ambiental*) (EIS) may be favourable, favourable with conditions or unfavourable, and will be based on the assessment of the environmental impacts involved at different phases of the project's development. However, if the decision is unfavourable, the procedure shall be extinguished.

[247] However, if the decision is favourable but subject to conditions, the EIS will set the conditions for the implementation of the project, the relevant studies and elements to be provided by the proposing entity, and the measures required to minimise and compensate for the negative environmental impacts. The execution of the project will be monitored and audited by the EIA Authority.

[248] It should also be noted that if this procedure is carried out while the project is still in the preliminary study or preliminary project phase, the project remains subject to environmental conformity certification. For that purpose, the entity concerned must submit the intended execution project accompanied by the execution project environmental conformity report to the EIA Authority.

[249] Lastly, it should be stressed that there is legislation governing the exercise of industrial or farming activity, as well as consumer law, that may be of relevance.

2.8.3 Intellectual Property

[250] Portugal has been a member of the EU since the mid-1980s and an enthusiastic participant in most international intellectual property rights (IPR) treaties for over a century and a half. Consequently, the IPR regime in Portugal is very similar to and harmonised with that found in other EU countries.

[251] The procedure for registration, protection and enforcement of IPR in Portugal depends on the type of right in question.

[252] Pursuant to the Portuguese Copyright and Neighbouring Rights Code (*Código do Direito de Autor e dos Direitos Conexos*) (PCRC) Decree-Law No. 122/2000 of

4 July (which is also related to the protection of databases), and Decree-Law No. 252/94 of 20 October (which is related to the protection of computer programs), original creative works (i.e., creations linked to the literary, scientific, and artistic domains), software and databases are protected by copyright irrespective of any registration or other formality.

[253] However, registration is possible, particularly for the purpose of obtaining evidence of ownership and of the date and creation of such ownership. In short, as in other EU countries, the protection of copyright in Portugal is fairly easy and automatic.

[254] As a general rule, if a third party wishes to use a copyright-protected work, written consent from the copyright owner is required.

[255] Consequently, if someone uses copyright-protected works or neighbouring rights without the consent of the right holder, that person may commit a crime of usurpation in accordance with the PCRC. The infringer may also be civilly liable for damages caused to the right holder. The three-step test and other exceptions to exclusive copyright are also applicable in Portugal.

[256] The enforcement of copyrights and neighbouring rights can be done through means similar to those that exist in other EU countries. In other words, the right holder may initiate an infringement action to require cessation of the infringing activity and may request indemnification for damages caused. In urgent proceedings, a preliminary injunction can also be requested.

[257] Portuguese law also considers some copyright infringement as a crime. The right holder can file a complaint with the public prosecutor or the Portuguese police, or the competent administrative authority (*Inspeção Geral das Atividades Culturais* – IGAC) regarding the infringement of such rights.

[258] Portuguese industrial property rights (e.g., designs, patents, trademarks) are protected upon registration at the *Instituto Nacional da Propriedade Industrial* (INPI). This protection is effective *erga omnes* and prevents the relevant design, invention or distinctive sign from, *inter alia*, being used, produced or marketed by others without the right holder's authorisation.

[259] The administrative registration procedures of industrial property rights at INPI are similar to those that exist at other European national patent and trademark offices. If the decision is unfavourable, the applicant has up to two months to appeal against the decision of INPI. The applicant can also resort to the ARBITRARE, the competent arbitration centre, in these matters.

[260] If a Portuguese trademark is granted, it will be protected for an initial period of ten years, counting from the application date and may be renewed indefinitely thereafter. A Portuguese patent is valid for a maximum period of twenty years from the date of its application. To maintain a patent in force, it is necessary to pay an annual fee which only needs to be paid from the fifth year onwards. Portuguese designs have a maximum validity of twenty-five years.

[261] Industrial property rights can be assigned or licensed through written agreements. In order to be effective vis-à-vis third parties, the agreements need to be recorded with INPI.

[262] Industrial property rights infringements can also lead to criminal offences as well as giving rise to civil liability (civil claims may lie from third parties owning the relevant registered industrial property rights). The enforcement of industrial property rights can be made through a complaint of the criminal offence to the public prosecutor or to the police (namely the *Autoridade de Segurança Alimentar e Económica* – ASAE). The owner of an industrial property right also has the possibility, in accordance with Portuguese law, of requesting a preliminary injunction at the competent court, namely the Portuguese Intellectual Property Court (*Tribunal da Propriedade Industrial*), to ensure the respect and non-infringement of the threatened IPR.

[263] In general terms, the registered IPRs of an entity are easy to analyse in a due diligence context. Unregistered copyrights and other rights, such as know-how and trade secrets, are hard to verify in a due diligence process. It is usual to request a list of the IPRs owned by the entity to be purchased/sold or subject to an investment, as well as documents and copies of all rights certificates related thereto, including proof of renewal payments.

[264] The assessment of the validity and ownership of the IPR used by the entity to be purchased/sold or which is subject to an investment is usually one of the most important issues to analyse. The validity and ownership of industrial property rights can normally be confirmed through searches made in INPI's public databases.

[265] Also, for the purpose of verifying the ownership and entitlement to copyrights used by the entity concerned (e.g., software, databases, scientific, literary and artistic works), it is normal to request a list of all authorisations, consent letters and other statements provided to the entity by third parties (i.e., including employees and founders of the relevant entity), or vice versa, as well as authorisations and licences provided by collective rights entities.

2.8.4 Distribution Agreements

[266] Within the meaning normally attributed to the term by Portuguese legal doctrine, the following types of contracts usually fall into the category of 'distribution agreements' (*contratos de distribuição*), namely commercial agency, concession and franchise agreements.

[267] The only type of distribution agreement that is specifically regulated by Portuguese law is the commercial agency contract (*contrato de agência*). Nonetheless, in view of the usual similarity between agency agreements and concession and franchise agreements, Portuguese case law and doctrine tend to apply to the latter by analogy with the legal provisions set out in the so-called Agency Act – i.e., Decree-Law No. 178/86 of 3 July (which transposed the Directive No. 86/653/CEE), as amended by Decree-Law No. 118/93 of 13 April.

[268] The termination rules established in the Agency Act are mandatory, regardless of the law chosen by the parties to govern the contract, to the extent that the agreement is predominantly executed in Portugal and to the extent that Portuguese law is more favourable for the agent.

[269] Under these rules, upon the termination of the agreement, the agent (and, by analogy, possibly other distributors) may be entitled to (i) compensation for the absence or insufficient advance notice of termination and (ii) client or goodwill compensation (*indemnização de clientela*). Goodwill indemnity aims to compensate the agent, once the contract is terminated (for any reason), for the benefits that the principal will probably continue to receive from customers introduced or developed by the agent. This compensation does not depend on proof of damage suffered by the agent since the more important issue to consider is the benefits accruing to the principal (which have occurred or are likely to occur) and which, having been common to both parties during the term of the contract, will be used only by the principal (or by its new counterpart) when the contract ends. Goodwill compensation will not apply in cases where termination is caused by the agent.

[270] The extension of this compensatory mechanism, by analogy, to other distribution agreements (such as concession and franchise agreements), and the extent to which compensation is required when it is so applied, is subject to debate in Portuguese doctrine and jurisprudence.

[271] The Portuguese legal framework for insurance distribution (approved by Law No. 7/2019, of 16 January, which, among other aspects, implemented IDD II into Portuguese law) includes a specific provision on goodwill compensation (*indemnização de clientela*).

[272] According to this law, goodwill compensation is an indemnity provided in Portuguese law to compensate insurance intermediaries in case of termination of their respective insurance distribution agreements (in which cases the insurance policies become direct insurance policies). The indemnity is due when the intermediary: (i) acquired new customers for the insurance undertaking; or (ii) substantially increased the volume of business from existing clients, and the insurance undertaking benefits, after the termination of the agreement, from the business developed by the insurance intermediary. The minimum amount provided for in the law for this indemnity corresponds to twice the average annual remuneration of the insurance intermediary in the previous five years or during the years the agreement was actually in force (if less than five).

[273] The goodwill compensation is not due in cases where the agreement was terminated by the insurance intermediary without cause or by the insurance undertaking with cause ('cause' in this case, meaning behaviour by the other party to the agreement which, due to its severity and consequences, makes it immediately and practically impossible to continue the contractual relationship). The goodwill compensation will also not be due in circumstances where the insurance intermediary has assigned its contractual position with the agreement of the insurance undertaking.

2.8.5 Valuation

[274] The valuation of IPR, brands and goodwill is an extremely complex matter, and there are no established methodologies used in Portugal. Indeed, valuations can adopt several different approaches. When performing a valuation, the existence of burdens, liens and infringement proceedings may lead to a decrease in market value. IPR are temporary rights, and therefore the remaining duration of exclusivity has a significant impact on the value.

2.8.6 Change of Control Clauses

[275] Change of control provisions is commonly used. When set out in contractual arrangements, they usually require prior consents from the relevant counterparty(ies) or from regulators, financing entities and suppliers, in the absence of which they may cause an event of default.

[276] The most common form of corporate financing in Portugal is still debt (rather than equity). Banking plays a very important role in the leverage of Portuguese companies, so it is not at all uncommon for banks to impose change of control clauses. Nonetheless, it is rare for banks to raise obstacles to M&A transactions, provided that their consent or waiver is requested prior to closing.

2.9 The Due Diligence Process

[277] 'Due diligence' is a normal process in the Portuguese M&A market, regardless of the level of sophistication of the transaction. It is customary to review and audit key aspects of the business such as commercial, financial, tax, labour, property planning and environmental, these being essential to the legal drafting of the transaction documents and playing a significant contractual role in terms of representations, warranties and indemnities, which are both common and enforceable. In fact, given that the most common obstacle to a successful M&A transaction is the information gap between sellers and buyers, this may lead to a relatively long and thorough process of due diligence, which in turn automatically leads to lengthier negotiations over representations and warranties. For example, when the acquisition of real estate is a critical factor, access to public records is essential, not only for confirmation purposes but also to assess whether there are any matters that may affect the transaction, such as registered rights, restrictions, or charges, including mortgages, easements, or encumbrances on the property.

[278] For high-level transactions in Portugal, sellers are perfectly accustomed to the requirement for due diligence in respect of any number of matters pertaining to the specific business. Even in mid-level transactions, sellers in Portugal are likely to expect a potential purchaser to conduct a review of several aspects of the business/asset that is being targeted.

[279] In recent years, there has been an increase in reviews and surveys covering environmental issues, particularly those relating to asbestos and soil analysis. Portuguese sellers are likely to expect environmental inspections from a purchaser, and that is why, in some situations, sellers will provide their own environmental assessment in advance.

[280] In high-level transactions, virtual data rooms are often used.

[281] The vendor is naturally exposed to risk where it becomes the object of due diligence and auditing and thus needs to share documents and negotiate with counterparties that may not adopt the same levels of security and care. Thus, apart from preparing for external threats, companies must also internally control the information disclosed during a negotiation process.

[282] As for legal practice, technology in the deal-making process has become increasingly important. Companies are generally more aware of it and have been acting accordingly. It seems that the days of a physical data room, paper format, traditional post mail and the deployment of large teams are gone, particularly in cross-border M&A deal-making. Nowadays, companies with even a minimal level of sophistication are aided by specialised software and IT companies in order to guarantee accurate information disclosure in the context of M&A transactions.

[283] In June 2018, Morais Leitão agreed to a deal with Luminance for the provision of artificial intelligence (AI) software that uses pattern recognition algorithms, statistical probability analysis and machine learning to analyse documents. Once documents are uploaded, algorithms identify clauses, extract data and highlight anomalies. Since that time, Luminance has been used in several transactions, adding value to lawyers' work but without replacing a lawyer's analysis, perception and creativity.

2.10 Role of the Courts

[284] Portuguese courts play an important role in the resolution of disputes in Portugal. In general terms, they decide with independence and impartiality. The decisions of lower courts may be appealed to higher courts. However, as compared with other European courts, the Portuguese courts are generally not considered to be the fastest to decide.

[285] With respect to alternative methods of dispute resolution, it is worth noting that arbitration has gained greater acceptance over the years as a way of resolving disputes in Portugal. Arbitration is particularly advantageous for settling disputes of a special technical nature or of greater complexity since arbitrators can be selected having regard to their particular skills and knowledge of the subject matter of the dispute, whereas Portuguese judges are selected randomly. Finally, arbitration is usually a much faster way of resolving disputes than resorting to State courts.

[286] Disputes arising from contractual provisions (e.g., restrictive covenants, confidentiality constraints to ensure data privacy, protection of minority shareholder

rights, enforcement of warranties or claims for damages) may be settled through the Portuguese courts. However, as mentioned above, when the subject matter of dispute has a very technical nature, it may be preferable to settle it through arbitration.

[287] In addition, it should be noted that legal proceedings in Portugal are usually public, whereas, in arbitration, the parties may stipulate that the arbitration procedure is to be confidential. This issue is highly relevant because sometimes companies, for reputational or business reasons, do not want it made public that they are involved in a particular dispute.

[288] Finally, it is worth mentioning that in 2018, the Portuguese Government approved a legislative draft on intra-corporate arbitration based on a draft regime prepared by the Portuguese Arbitration Association (*Associação Portuguesa de Arbitragem*). The legislative draft governs arbitration clauses inserted in the articles of association of companies with registered offices in Portugal, although some have commented that the legal regime could also be applicable to foreign companies if certain requirements are met.

3 MERGER CONTROLS: ANTITRUST/ COMPETITION ISSUES

3.1 Relevant Legislation and Competent Authorities

3.1.1 Merger Control in Portugal

[289] One of the key legal issues to consider in an M&A transaction is competition law, particularly merger control. In this context, a transaction may fall within the scope of merger control on account of potential implications for the relevant market structure, relevant changes or acquisitions of market shares by the parties involved in the transaction, or other competition effects in the market.

[290] In such cases, the parties are likely to incur merger control obligations, namely mandatory notification to the competent authority, which may affect the feasibility, timetable, cost and other practical considerations of the transaction.

[291] Depending on its configuration and specifications, a transaction may fall within the scope of EU or Portuguese merger control and even of other merger control regimes where the transaction may produce 'effects' (so-called foreign-to-foreign transactions).

[292] A transaction may fall within the scope of EU merger control, specifically of Council Regulation (EU) No. 139/2004 of 20 January (the '**EU Merger Regulation**'). This may be applicable to a concentration with an EU dimension that exceeds applicable jurisdictional thresholds. Transactions falling within the scope of the EU Merger Regulation must be notified (and should be pre-notified) to the European Commission. Generally, when a transaction falls within the scope of EU merger control provisions, this will preclude the application of national merger control law in any Member State of the EU, including Portugal, without prejudice to the mutual referral provisions contemplated by the EU Merger Regulation.

[293] Conversely, if a transaction does not fall within the scope of the EU Merger Regulation, Portuguese merger control may still apply if the jurisdictional thresholds in Portugal are met, as explained below.

[294] Merger control is enforced in Portugal by the AdC, established in 2003, in terms of its by-laws approved by Decree-Law No. 125/2014 of 18 August, amended lastly by Law No. 17/2022 of 17 August. The AdC is an administrative authority with investigative, regulatory and sanctioning powers to enforce competition law in Portugal, including rules on merger control.

[295] The relevant legislation enforced by the AdC in respect of merger control is Law No. 19/2012 of 8 May, amended lastly by Law No. 17/2022 of 17 August ('Competition Act'), which provides the jurisdictional thresholds determining the obligation for mandatory filing of a transaction. The law also details the procedure for the competition assessment of the transaction and, also, establishes a mandatory suspension obligation (the so-called stand-still obligation), according to which a transaction that is subject to mandatory filing cannot be completed (i) without prior notification; and (ii) before the adoption by the AdC of an express or tacit decision of non-opposition to the transaction. Furthermore, as we will detail below, the Competition Act envisages severe legal consequences for failure to comply with this stand-still obligation.

3.1.2 Merger Notification

[296] A transaction is subject to mandatory filing with the AdC if it meets the jurisdictional thresholds of the Competition Act.

[297] First, the transaction must constitute a 'concentration' that produces a change of control on a lasting basis over the whole of an undertaking or part of it, following the EU Merger Regulation and the European Commission's practice very closely.

[298] Such a change of control may take place through (but not limited to) a merger between two or more undertakings, the acquisition, directly or indirectly, of control over one or more undertakings, and even through the creation of a full-function joint venture.

[299] Control, in this sense, is deemed as the ability to exercise decisive influence over an undertaking's activity. Therefore, the acquisition of control may consist of the acquisition of the whole or part of the share capital or of the assets of one or more undertakings or the acquisition of any rights that grant decisive influence over the composition and decision-making of an undertaking.[6]

[6] Please *see* Art. 36(3) of the Competition Act. Moniz, Carlos Botelho (coord.), *Lei da Concorrência Anotada*, Almedina, 2016, p. 356.

[300] In fact, the acquisition of a minority share position can still constitute a relevant concentration to this effect if, in practice, it confers control on the acquirer, namely the right to exercise, alone or jointly with other undertakings, control over the acquired company.[7]

[301] Nonetheless, the Competition Act specifically excludes from the concept of concentration: (i) the acquisition of shareholdings or assets by an insolvency administrator in the context of insolvency proceedings; (ii) the acquisition of shareholdings by way of a mere guarantee; and (iii) the temporary acquisition by financial institutions or insurance companies of shareholdings of companies outside of the financial sector and only for resale purposes, as long as the acquisition is not concluded on a lasting basis, the shareholders do not exercise the voting rights inherent to those shareholdings for the purpose of determining the competitive behaviour of the undertakings concerned, or do exercise those rights for the purpose of disposing of those shareholdings, which must occur within one year of the acquisition of the shareholdings in question.

[302] Furthermore, in the context of bank recapitalisation and resolution, Law No. 63-A/2008 of 24 November and Decree-Law No. 298/92 of 31 December have established that the acquisition by the Portuguese State of a controlling shareholding in a credit institution or the transfer of its business to a transition bank as ordered by the Bank of Portugal is also excluded from the scope of merger control in Portugal.[8]

[303] Second, and once established that a transaction constitutes a concentration for the purposes of the Competition Act, it will be subject to a mandatory merger notification and competition assessment by the AdC if one of the following alternative thresholds is met:

(i) *Turnover threshold*: if, in the preceding year, the aggregate combined turnover of the undertakings involved in the transaction in Portugal exceeded EUR100 000 000.00, after the deduction of taxes directly related to turnover, provided that the individual turnover achieved in Portugal in the same period by at least two of these undertakings exceeded EUR5 000 000.00.
(ii) *Standard market share threshold*: if the implementation of the transaction results in the acquisition, creation or reinforcement of a market share exceeding 50% in the relevant market or in a substantial part of it.
(iii) *De minimis market share threshold*: even if there is only a creation or reinforcement of a share between 30% and 50% of the relevant market, the transaction will be subject to mandatory notification if at least two of the participating undertakings achieved individually in Portugal a turnover of at least EUR5 000 000.00 in the previous year.

[304] In respect of the market share threshold, it must be noted that the AdC takes account only of the market share of undertakings in Portugal, even if the relevant

[7] Porto, Manuel Lopes et al. (coord.), *Lei da Concorrência – Comentário Conimbricense*, Almedina, 2017, p. 514.

[8] Moniz, Carlos Botelho (coord.), *supra*, p. 371, Porto, Manuel Lopes et al. (coord.), *supra*, p. 519.

geographic market is wider in scope.[9] The scope of this jurisdictional threshold is thus defined very broadly by the AdC.

[305] For instance, if the operation encompasses a mere transfer of a market position (the acquirer not having been present in the relevant market of the target company prior to the conclusion of the transaction), the operation is still envisaged as an 'acquisition of market share' by the AdC. Therefore, if the target has a market share over 50% or 30% in a relevant product market in Portugal (in this last case, if at least two of the participating undertakings had a turnover in excess of EUR5 000 000.00), the operation must be notified to the AdC.[10]

[306] In fact, even in a case where there is no substantive overlap, merger control rules may apply if just one of the thresholds is met. Where there is no substantive overlap and no competition concerns, the notification may follow the simplified (and quicker) procedure (the Short Form procedure).

[307] Also, there is no *de minimis* exception in regard to the market share threshold, which means that if the acquirer has a market share over 50% or 30% in a relevant product market in Portugal and if the target has a residual market share in that market (even if less than 1%), this operation must also be notified to the AdC.[11]

[308] Additionally, a transaction may be subject to notification before the Competition AdC even if the target company has been recently created and has had no economic activity prior to or at the time of the notification if the AdC considers that, in view of the estimated market share of the company in the future (accounting, *inter alia*, for its estimated capacity), there will be a reinforcement of market share for the acquirer that is above the 50% limb.[12]

[309] Finally, in case of the creation or a change of control over a joint venture which has a market share over 50% or 30% in a given relevant product market in Portugal (e.g., if one of the parent companies acquires sole control over the company), such an operation will be subject to notification to the AdC.[13]

[310] It should also be noted that where two or more transactions, which individually would not be subject to notification, are executed within a period of two years and between the same parties, these may be regarded as a single transaction and subject to mandatory filing in circumstances where the jurisdictional thresholds are met.[14]

---

[9] Moniz, Carlos Botelho (coord.), *supra*, p. 382.

[10] *See* Cases Ccent. 38/2009, *Suntory/Black Lion*, Ccent. 10/2011, *Lonsen/Kiri Singapore*, Ccent. 42/2011, *Sagard/Negócio de Massa Refrigerada da Sara Lee*; Porto, Manuel Lopes et al. (coord.), *supra*, p. 526.

[11] *See* Case Ccent. 16/2005, *Enernova/Ortiga-Safra*, Porto, Manuel Lopes et al. (coord.), *supra*, p. 527.

[12] Please *see* cases Ccent. 18/2004 *Secil Britas/Carburos* and Ccent. 16/2005 *Enernova/Oritga-Safra*. Porto, Manuel Lopes et al. (coord.), *supra*, footnote 13.

[13] *See* Cases Ccent. 13/2003, *CSN/Corus/Lusosider*, Ccent. 37/2004, *Barraqueiro/Arriva*, Ccent. 36/2006, *Ciba/Raisio*, Ccent. 38/2003, *Arriva/TST*, Ccent. 5/2012, *Hearst**Fimalac/Fitch*; Porto, Manuel Lopes et al. (coord.), *supra*, p. 527.

[14] Please *see* Art. 38(1) of the Competition Act. Also *see* Case Ccent. 15/2008, *TOP Atlântico/Ativos Policarpo**Ativos Portimar*.

[311] In a foreign merger, where both undertakings or the target has, directly or indirectly, sales in Portugal (even though they are not established in Portugal) and meet the jurisdictional thresholds, the operation may be subject to mandatory filing in Portugal. A so-called foreign-to-foreign transaction may fall within the scope of the Competition Act in these cases to the extent that the merger has or may have effects in the territory of Portugal.

[312] Where a transaction is subject to mandatory filing and the parties fail to comply with the obligations set out in the law, either by not notifying the transaction to the AdC, by concluding a transaction without an express or tacit non-opposition decision or in breach of a prohibition decision by the AdC, the parties may incur severe sanctions for breaching merger control law.

[313] On the one hand, the AdC may impose heavy fines both on the undertakings concerned and on the board members and managers of such undertakings. Where merger control law is breached, the undertakings concerned may be liable for fines of up to 10% of the previous year's turnover of each of the participating undertakings, and the board members and managers[15] of such undertakings can be personally liable for the undertaking's infringement (if it was, or ought to have been, within their knowledge) and may be subject to fines of up to 10% of their annual income.

[314] On the other hand, a failure to comply with the merger control rules may affect the legal validity of the transaction itself. A transaction subject to mandatory filing concluded without the required notification or before a tacit or express non-opposition decision has been issued by the AdC is invalid and of no legal effect.[16] If a transaction is implemented after a prohibition decision by the AdC, it is null and void and may be so declared by a court in proceedings brought by a private party (e.g., by a competitor or a client).

[315] Additionally, the Competition Act confers on the AdC powers to conduct ex officio investigations into concentrations implemented in the previous five years in violation of the Competition Act and may order the parties to notify such deals.[17] By way of penalty, the Competition Act envisages that the filing fees will increase to double the amount originally due and confers power on the AdC to apply a periodic penalty payment of up to 5% of the average daily turnover of the preceding year for each day of delay. In the context of these investigations, the AdC is empowered to take measures in order to restore the situation that existed prior to the concentration, notably the split of the merged undertakings or assets, including the reversal of the operation or termination of the situation of control.

---

15 In this case, the Competition Act in Art. 73(6) means the persons holding positions in the managing bodies heading or being responsible for the supervision of the relevant department where the infraction is carried out. Porto, Manuel Lopes et al. (coord.), *supra*, p. 840.

16 Please *see* Art. 40(6) of the Competition Act and Case Ccent. 47/2009, *Farminvest/ParaRede*.

17 *See* Art. 56(1) of the Competition Act. Such ex officio investigations may also be conducted by the Authority if the non-opposition decision was based on false or incorrect information provided by the undertakings involved in the merger filing of the transaction or even if the parties disregard conditions or obligations imposed by the AdC. Please *see* Art. 57(1)(b) of the Competition Act.

3.2 Merger Control Process

[316] A transaction may be notified to the AdC after the conclusion of an agreement or following the announcement to the market of takeover bids, exchange offers or acquisitions of control over companies with shares admitted to trading on a regulated market or of the decision to award a public contract.

[317] The Competition Act also provides the possibility of voluntary filing for parties to a concentration which demonstrates serious intent to conclude an agreement or to publicly announce a public bid if such an agreement or public offer may constitute a concentration within the scope of merger control.

[318] Nonetheless, the Competition Act, following the European Commission's practice, also envisages the possibility of prior assessment of the concentration in pre-notification contacts. These may be helpful where there is doubt about the obligation to notify, the applicability of the relevant jurisdictional thresholds in a given transaction, or the availability of the short-form notification process. It can also help to expedite the filing proceedings, especially in more complex transactions, where informal and confidential contacts can be made to discuss issues of potential concern to the AdC, such as the definition of the relevant market, the existence of competition concerns and the viability of ancillary constraints. Although these informal contacts may help to minimise the need for requests for additional information during the AdC's assessment of the concentration (and may thus help to expedite the proceedings), the AdC will usually only provide legal certainty regarding these issues following formal notification of the transaction. This is a factor that may, in practice, deter the parties from engaging in pre-notification contacts with the AdC.

[319] Following notification of a concentration to the AdC, the procedure for its assessment may be subject to two phases: an initial investigation (Phase 1) and an in-depth investigation (Phase 2).

[320] The notification becomes effective upon payment of the filing fees by the parties concerned and, if the information provided is not considered incomplete by the AdC, within seven working days of its receipt.[18] After it becomes effective, the AdC, within five working days, publishes a summary of the notification in two national newspapers, at the expense of the notifying parties, and on its website so that any third party with a legitimate right or interest who may be affected by the transaction may present its comments within the timeframe set by the AdC (usually ten working days).

[321] Once the notification is deemed complete by the AdC, it has thirty working days to reach one of the following decisions: (i) that the concentration is not subject to notification; (ii) not to oppose the concentration when it considers that the operation, as notified, is not liable to create significate impediments to effective

[18] *See* Art. 45(1) of the Competition Act. If the AdC deems the notification incomplete, the parties are asked to correct or complete it and it will only be effective upon new analysis of the notification, which would invariably delay the competition assessment and the eventual non-opposition decision.

competition (with or without commitments offered by the parties); or (iii) to initiate an in-depth investigation (a Phase 2 investigation), where it finds that the concentration, as notified and in light of the elements and documentation provided, raises serious concerns as to its ability to deter effective competition.

[322] In case the AdC does not reach a decision within this thirty-working day timeframe, and this deadline has not been suspended, the concentration is deemed to have been tacitly cleared by the AdC.

[323] In case the AdC decides to initiate an in-depth investigation, it has ninety working days, counting from the date the notification was considered effective by the AdC, to conclude the in-depth investigation (in practice, assuming the AdC exhausts the thirty-working day period in Phase 1, it will have sixty extra working days to reach its conclusion in a Phase 2 investigation).

[324] At the end of Phase 2 proceedings, the AdC may reach one of these decisions: (i) not to oppose the concentration when it considers that the operation, as notified, is not liable to create significant impediments to effective competition (with or without commitments offered by the parties); or (ii) prohibit the concentration when it considers that it is liable to create significant impediments to effective competition in the national market or in a substantial part of it. Where the concentration has already been concluded, the AdC must determine adequate measures for the reestablishment of effective competition, notably through the unbundling of the merged undertakings or assets, including the reversal of the operation or the termination of control.

[325] If the AdC does not reach a decision within this timeframe and if this deadline has not been suspended, the rule explained previously also applies to the in-depth investigation phase, and the concentration is deemed to have been tacitly cleared by the AdC.

[326] Even though the Competition Act defines strict deadlines for the AdC to issue a decision in both the initial and in-depth investigation phases, as detailed above, it also envisages the possibility of suspension of these deadlines. In practice, this means that if there are any circumstances that allow for a suspension of the deadline, the thirty- or ninety-working-day deadlines for a tacit decision of non-opposition are extended.

[327] These deadlines can be suspended for three reasons: (i) a request for additional information, whether in the initial or the in-depth investigation; (ii) the submission of commitments, also in both phases of the assessment; and (iii) hearing of the notifying parties and of third parties.

[328] Three important practical comments may be made. First, regarding requests by the AdC for additional information, the parties can be requested to provide further clarifications, documentation or correction of information already filed if these are considered necessary for the proper analysis of the concentration. This request for additional information suspends the decision deadline until the information and/or documentation has been provided by the notifying parties. In practice, this means that if there are requests for additional information (which is quite frequent in the AdC's practice), the thirty- and ninety-working-day deadlines for a non-opposition decision are extended, and the date planned for implementation of the transaction is delayed.

[329] Second, the notifying parties in both the initial investigation and the in-depth investigation phases may submit voluntary undertakings/commitments designed to mitigate any competition concerns the AdC may express during its assessment of the concentration. Any such submission of commitments by the parties suspends the decision deadline, in this case, for twenty working days. This twenty-working day suspension is established for the purpose of allowing negotiations to take place between the parties and the AdC regarding the configuration and merits of the commitments proposed. The deadline only resumes once the AdC notifies the parties that the commitments have been accepted or refused.

[330] Third, the Competition Act establishes that in both the initial and the in-depth investigation phases, before the AdC reaches a decision, it must notify the notifying parties and interested third parties of their draft decision and must give the opportunity for these parties to be heard on it and to present their views on it. To this end, the parties must be provided with not less than a ten-working-day deadline to submit their considerations. During this time, the decision deadline is also suspended.

[331] It should be noted that third parties will only have the right to be heard if they have presented observations with a reasoned demonstration of their position regarding the operation. In such cases, if the interested third parties do not have access to the file on the concerning concentration, the deadline for the submission of considerations is extended to twenty working days.

[332] Nonetheless, in cases where there are no interested third parties wishing to present their observations regarding the concentration, and the AdC is about to issue an unconditional clearance decision, the AdC may choose not to hear the notifying parties, and consequently, the decision deadline is not suspended on this ground.

[333] Apart from being obliged to hear the considerations of interested third parties to the concentration, the AdC must, before deciding, hear other relevant regulatory authorities where the concentration in question is subject to sectoral regulation, namely in the banking and financial services or securities markets, or in the insurance, energy, communications, water and waste sectors. However, generally speaking, the opinion of the relevant regulatory authority is not binding on the AdC,[19] and it does not suspend the decision deadline as in the cases previously mentioned.

[334] Regarding the timing of a public offer to purchase or of an exchange offer that has been notified to the AdC, this can be implemented before the AdC's non-opposition decision insofar as the acquirer does not exercise the voting rights

[19] Except on the media sector, which specifically establishes in the attributions of ERC that its negative opinions in the context of merger control are binding on the AdC. For this case, please *see* Case Ccent. 41/2009, *Ongoing/Prisa/Media Capital*.

attaching to the relevant shareholdings or if such voting rights are only exercised in order to protect the full value of its investment. In this case, the AdC may grant a waiver of the stand-still obligation upon a reasoned request presented by the notifying parties, whether before or after the filing. This derogation may be granted in light of the consequences for the concerned parties of the suspension of the concentration or of the exercise of voting rights and the negative effects of the derogation on effective competition, in which case the AdC may award the derogation subject to conditions and obligations designed to safeguard the competition concerns that may arise.[20]

3.2.1 Competition Assessment of the Concentration

[335] The Competition Act provides that the purpose of merger control is to determine the effects of the transaction on the competition structure in order to preserve and develop effective competition in the national market or in a substantial part of it in the interest of intermediate and final consumers.

[336] Therefore, the Competition Act establishes that the criterion for the assessment of a concentration's compatibility with competition law is its potential to create significant impediments to effective competition in the national market or in a substantial part of it. Insofar as concentrations are deemed to create serious hindrances to effective competition, notably as a result of the creation or reinforcement of a dominant position in the relevant market, they ought not to be cleared by the AdC.

[337] To date, the Competition AdC has only prohibited the implementation of six concentrations:

(i) Case Ccent. 37/2004, Arriva/Barraqueiro, decision of 25 November 2004.
(ii) Case Ccent. 45/2004 Petrogal/Esso, decision of 15 December 2005.
(iii) Case Ccent. 22/2005, Brisa/AEO/AEE, decision of 5 April 2006.
(iv) Case Ccent. 12/2009, TAP/SPDH, decision of 19 November 2009.
(v) Case Ccent. 41/2009 Ongoing/Vertix/MediaCapital, decision of 30 March 2010.
(vi) Case Ccent 4/2013 Controlinvest/ZON Optimus/PT, decision of 31 July 2014.

[338] Usually, a prohibition decision will be justified by serious concerns about potential distortion of effective competition, namely by the creation or reinforcement of a dominant position or the creation of serious barriers to the entry of new competitors into the relevant market, and such a decision would, as a general rule, be reasoned in writing based on competition grounds.

[20] Nonetheless, the AdC has interpreted this provision very restrictively and has only conceded such a derogation in Case Ccent. 11/2010, *Triton/Grupo Stabilus*, §§10–12, a case of imminent insolvency of the company. In most cases, the AdC has rejected the requests of the parties for such a derogation. Please *see* cases Ccent. 12/2005, *Alliance Unichem/Alloga*, §25, Ccent. 24/2005, *Invescaima/Portucel Tejo*, §21, Ccent. 11/2006, *Grupo de Gestores UEE – Ibersuizas – Vistas Desarollo/UEE*, §31.

[339] However, there is an example of a case (*Ongoing/Vertix/Media Capital*, Ccent. 41/2009) which was prohibited based on a negative binding opinion of the regulatory authority for the media sector. In this case, the concentration was not prohibited based on competition grounds but on public interest concerns, namely freedom of speech and the diversity and plurality of the media.[21]

[340] In this context, if in the course of the competition assessment of the concentration, the AdC conveys significant concerns regarding the compatibility of the transaction with competition, the notifying parties may, at any time, submit voluntary commitments to the AdC to ensure the maintenance of effective competition. These commitments consist of changes to the transaction proposed by the notifying parties, which aim to resolve some of the AdC's competition concerns regarding the transaction and which allow the AdC to issue a decision of non-opposition to the concentration.

[341] These commitments may aim to create the necessary conditions for the entry of a new competitor or to reinforce the position of existing competitors and thereby prevent the creation or reinforcement of a dominant position or the lessening of competition on the relevant market.[22]

[342] According to the AdC and as a general rule, these commitments must be capable of immediate implementation and be effective in the short term and should, in principle, not require any type of monitoring or follow-up.[23] Moreover, these commitments usually correspond to the disposal of one or more assets which carry on their economic activity on an autonomous basis so that the divestment may mitigate or even eliminate the competition concern identified by the AdC in its assessment.[24]

[343] The AdC has accepted, as a commitment, the disinvestment of companies,[25] shareholdings,[26] intellectual property rights[27] and various assets,[28] the closing of certain areas of sale[29] and temporary assignment in the energy sector.[30]

---

[21] *See* Case Ccent. 41/2009, *Ongoing/Vertix/Media Capital*, §§ 35, 38 and 39.

[22] Moniz, Carlos Botelho (coord.), *supra*, p. 535; Case Ccent. 15/2006, *BCP/BPI*, § 2524; Case Ccent. 79/2007, *Transdev/Joalto*, § 305 and AdC, *Linhas de Orientacão sobre a adopcão de compromissos em control de concentracões*, 28 July 2011. Available at http://www.concorrencia.pt/SiteCollectionDocuments/Noticias_e_Eventos/Comunicados/Comunicado201109_DOC_2-Linhas_de_Orientacao.pdf, last accessed on 3 July 2020, §§ 41–45.

[23] Moniz, Carlos Botelho (coord.), *supra*, p. 536; Case Ccent. 15/2006, *BCP/BPI*, § 2524; Case Ccent. 79/2007, *Transdev/Joalto*, § 305.

[24] Moniz, Carlos Botelho (coord.), *supra*, p. 536.

[25] *See* Case Ccent. 16/2004, *Caixa Seguros/BCP Seguros*, § 550.

[26] *See* Case Ccent 8/2006, *Sonae/PT* and Case Ccent. 15/2006, *BCP/BPI*.

[27] *See* Case Ccent. 22/2008, *Sumolis/Compal*; Case Ccent. 25/2010, *Johnson/Sara Lee*.

[28] *See* Case Ccent. 51/2007, *Sonae/Carrefour*; Case Ccent. 1/2008, *Pingo Doce/Plus*, Case Ccent.40/2010, *Bencom/Ativos BPI*.

[29] *See* Case Ccent. 51/2007, *Sonae/Carrefour*.

[30] *See* Case Ccent. 6/2008, *EDP/Ativos EDIA*.

[344] Despite the general preference for structural remedies, the AdC has also accepted several behavioural commitments such as access to services,[31]legal separation between companies,[32] price control,[33] non-discontinuation of activities,[34] stand-still obligations,[35] network effect mitigation[36]and the provision of free services,[37] among others.

3.2.2 Ancillary Restraints

[345] The Competition Act envisages that a non-opposition decision may include ancillary restrictions on competition which are considered directly related and necessary for the implementation of the concentration. This means that certain clauses included in the transaction's implementation agreements which may limit the action of the parties in the market and which could potentially be restrictive of competition may be authorised by the AdC in the scope of a non-opposition decision.[38]

[346] For an ancillary restriction to be treated as directly related to the implementation of a transaction, it has to be shown to be economically linked to the objective of the transaction and to have the purpose of allowing a smooth transition subsequent to the concentration.[39]

[347] The most frequent types of ancillary restrictions included in concentrations and which may be cleared by the AdC are the following:

(i) *Non-competition clauses*: these types of clauses are usually envisaged to allow the transfer and preservation of the value of the assets acquired in the transaction, mainly (but not limited to) the know-how acquired from the competing party. In the practice of the AdC, these clauses are normally authorised for a duration of no more than two or three years.[40] These clauses should also be limited in their material and geographic scope by reference to the goods or services and geographic area where the acquired company exercised its activity at the time of filing.[41]

31 *See* Case Ccent. 3/2004, *Lusomundo/Ocasião*, § 193; Case Ccent. 40/2010, *Bencom/BP Acores*, § 210.

32 *See* Case Ccent. 40/2003, *EDP/Portgás*, § 126.

33 *See* Case Ccent. 47/2003, *PPTV/PT Conteúdos/SportTV*, § 132; Case Ccent. 57/2006, *TAP/Portugália*.

34 *See* Case Ccent. 44/2003, *Drager/Hillenbrand*, § 69.

35 *See* Case Ccent. 1/2008, *Pingo Doce/Plus*, §§ 330, 341, 346; Case Ccent. 51/2007, *Sonae/Carrefour*.

36 *See* Case Ccent. 8/2006, *Sonae/PT*.

37 *See* Case Ccent. 15/2006, *BCP/BPI*.

38 Moniz, Carlos Botelho (coord.), *supra*, p. 463.

39 Moniz, Carlos Botelho (coord.), *supra*, pp. 463,464.

40 Please *see*, *e.g.*, Cases Ccent 21/2006, *Grupo Pestana/Intervisa*, §26, Ccent 19/2008, *Toyota Caetano/ Movicargo Industrial*, § 48 and 50, Ccent. 33/2009, *Auto Sueco/Arrábidaspecas*, §31; Moniz, Carlos Botelho (coord.), *supra*, p. 465. However, in certain, very limited and specific cases, the AdC has recognised a need for a special protection of the know-how and intellectual property rights acquired and has accepted an extended duration of non-competition clauses. Please *see* cases Ccent. 38/2008, *Explorer II/Probos*, §§ 45–49 and Ccent 23/2009, *Explorer II/Grupo Valor, §§ 43–48;* Moniz, Carlos Botelho (coord.), *supra*, pp. 465 and 466.

41 Moniz, Carlos Botelho (coord.), *supra*, p. 466.

(ii) *Non-competition clauses between parent companies and the joint venture*: these types of clauses are usually authorised for a more extensive period than in the previous case, including for the duration of the joint venture itself, as they aim to regulate the relationship between the parent companies and the joint venture and to ensure the goodwill of all parties involved in the sharing of know-how and access to the assets of all parties.[42]

(iii) *Obligations of non-solicitation of customers or employees of the acquired company*: these types of clauses are generally analysed in a similar way to non-competition clauses, as they have a similar aim, that is to protect a key part of the value acquired in the context of the transaction, namely the client contacts and human resources.[43]

(iv) *Supply, distribution, licensing and provision of transitional service agreements*: given the competition concerns that may arise from these types of clauses, which may sometimes be designed to create exclusivity obligations between the parties to the transaction,[44] such clauses will require a case-by-case analysis within the framework of the transaction for which they were envisaged.[45]

[348] Upon conclusion of the transaction, any behaviour restrictive of effective competition which is perpetrated within the Portuguese territory and which may be deemed an anti-competitive restrictive practice, such as the conclusion of agreements between undertakings, concerted practices and decision of association of undertakings which have as their object or effect a restriction on competition or the abuse of a dominant position in terms of Articles 9 and 10 of the Competition Act (expressed in similar terms to Articles 101 and 102 of the Treaty on the Functioning of the European Union), may be pursued by the AdC in a misdemeanours procedure and may result in the imposition of heavy fines.

3.3 Anti-competitive Restraints Applicable to Employees and Directors

3.3.1 Non-competitive Clauses in Employment Agreements

[349] According to the Portuguese Labour Code (*Código do Trabalho*) (PLC), the employee must, for the duration of his employment agreement, be loyal to his employer, namely by (i) not negotiating in his own name or on behalf of a third party in competition with the employer, or (ii) not disclosing information concerning the employer's organisation, methods of production or business.

[42] European Commission, *Commission Communication regarding restrictions directly related and necessary to concentrations*, 2005. Available at https://eur-lex.europa.eu/legal-content/EN/ALL/?uri=CELEX%3A52005XC0305%2802%29, last accessed in 3 Jul. 2020, §36, Moniz, Carlos Botelho (coord.), *supra*, p. 466, Porto, Manuel Lopes et al. (coord.), *supra*, p. 572.

[43] Moniz, Carlos Botelho (coord.), *supra*, p. 467, Porto, Manuel Lopes et al. (coord.), *supra*, p. 571.

[44] Please *see* cases Ccent. 3/2009, *Schwepps/Ativos CC*, §§ 89 and following and Ccent. 15/2009, *BASF Coatings/CIN Tintas*, §§ 59 and following.

[45] Please *see* Cases Ccent. 23/2007, *Tomgal/Idal*, §§12–23, Ccent. 9/2009, *Lallemand Bio/GBI Unipessoal/Mauri/GBI Bakery*, §48–53. Moniz, Carlos Botelho (coord.), *supra*, p. 467.

[350] Upon the termination of the contract, non-competition obligations as between employer and employee may only be applied once employer and employee have agreed on it and under strict legal constraints. Non-compete agreements are only lawful if made in writing, if the activity of the employee is likely to cause harm to the employer, and if a compensation amount is paid to the former employee during the non-competition period. As a general rule, the maximum duration of this period is two years. However, if the employee was assigned to an activity which by its fiduciary nature constituted a special relationship with the company or to an activity that gave the employee access to particularly sensitive information relevant to competition, the duration of the agreement may be increased to up to three years.

[351] Under Portuguese law, any agreements between employers which (i) prohibit the admission of an employee who worked for them, or (ii) stipulate the payment of an indemnity if that employee is engaged are null and void.

[352] Pursuant to Portuguese Labour Law, employees are free to terminate their employment contract, provided a prior notice (between fifteen and sixty days, depending on the type of contract and its duration) is given. Taking this into account, should a company wish to prevent the departure of a management team and/or of certain key employees, the renegotiation of labour conditions, permanence, and/or non-competition agreements are possible ways to consider.

3.3.2 Restrictions on Competitive Activities by Directors

[353] Pursuant to the PCC, restrictions apply to the carrying out of competitive activities by managers and directors if such activities falling within the company's purpose are being carried out by the company or where its exercise has been decided on by the shareholders.

[354] Regarding private limited liability companies by *quotas*, managers may not, without the consent of the partners, carry out (i) on their own account; or (ii) on behalf of others, an activity deemed competitive with that of the company. Carrying out an activity on their own includes (i) holding, directly or through an intermediary, participation in a company in which the manager is attributed with unlimited liability; or (ii) holding at least 20% of the share capital or profits of a company in which the manager is attributed with limited liability. However, consent is presumed if the exercise of the activity started prior to the manager's appointment and was known to partners holding the majority of the capital, as well as where knowledge of the manager's activity existed, and the manager continues to exercise his functions more than ninety days after a new activity of the company with which he is competing has been decided upon.

[355] In respect of limited liability companies by shares, except with authorisation by the general meeting (which must define the regime for access to sensitive information by the relevant director), directors may not carry out (i) on their own account; or (ii) on behalf of any other person an activity competing with that of the company; or (iii) be appointed on behalf of or in representation of a competing company.

[356] Breach of these constraints (whether in the case of limited liability companies by shares or private limited liability companies by *quotas*) constitutes just cause for termination, and the manager or director concerned is obliged to compensate the company for any losses suffered by it. Nevertheless, such company's rights expire ninety days from the time all shareholders became aware of the activity carried out by the manager/director or, in any case, within five years from the start of such activity.

4 TAXATION ASPECTS

4.1 Nature of the Tax Regime

[357] Although the Portuguese tax system fulfils all the most demanding international criteria as regards transparency, it can be characterised as uncertain, as it is exposed to very frequent changes in some important regimes, and it is too often affected by contradictory national case law. As for the tax rules, their degree of complexity does not seem to be higher than the average in developed countries; yet, there is a high level of litigation in tax matters which seems to originate more in the strict and sometimes aggressive stance adopted by the AT and by some taxpayers than in the intricacies of the law. From our point of view, law enforcement in the field of tax has become harsher in recent times.

4.2 Liability to Tax

[358] As a rule, a business vehicle is deemed to be subject to tax in Portugal if it is considered to be a resident taxpayer, i.e., when its legal seat or the place of effective management is located in that territory. Tax-resident corporate bodies are subject to tax on their worldwide income, regardless of the country of source of such income, and, in general, all deductible expenses are also taken into account.

[359] If a company is not resident for tax purposes but carries out its activity through a permanent establishment (*estabelecimento estável*) (PE) situated in Portugal, it will be liable to Portuguese tax in respect of all the income attributable to that PE. The taxable profit of the latter is, *mutatis mutandis*, determined according to the same rules as are applicable to resident companies.

[360] The general corporate income tax (*imposto sobre o rendimento de pessoas coletivas*) (IRC) rate applicable on the Portuguese mainland is 21% to resident entities and to non-residents with a PE therein (as well as withholding income tax – 'WHT', *retenção na fonte* – at the rate of 25% to non-residents). In the Madeira Archipelago and in the Azores, that rate lowers to 14.7%.

[361] Entities qualifying as small- or medium-sized enterprises (SMEs) are subject to a 17% rate which applies to the first EUR25 000.00 of taxable profits. The remaining profits are subject to the applicable general tax rates.

[362] A state surtax (*derrama estadual*) is applicable to a taxable profit of more than EUR1 500 000.00 (only for taxpayers on the Portuguese mainland) according to the following brackets:

(i) from EUR1 500 000.00 up to EUR7 500 000.00: 3%;
(ii) from EUR7 500 000.00 up to EUR35 000 000.00: 5%; and
(iii) on profits exceeding EUR35 000 000.00: 9%.

[363] Local surtax (*derrama municipal*) of up to 1.5% of taxable profits is levied by municipalities.

[364] Certain expenditures incurred by entities subject to IRC are separately subject to autonomous taxation (*tributação autónoma*), with tax rates ranging from 5% to 70% (the latter for non-documented expenses borne by a company exempt from IRC).

[365] In general, capital gains are considered items of the general taxable profits and are taxed at the general IRC rate. Capital losses may be deducted if the general deductibility rules are fulfilled, but not to the extent of profits or reserves distributed in previous years or capital gains realised from the disposal of shares that benefited from the participation exemption or from the foreign (indirect) tax credit.

4.2.1 Residents

[366] Under the participation exemption regime, capital gains and losses realised by Portuguese-resident companies from the disposal of shares and other equity items (e.g., the so-called supplementary capital contributions) are exempt, provided that the following requirements are met: (i) the company disposing of the shareholding must hold – directly and/or indirectly – at least 10% of the share capital or voting rights of an entity; (ii) such interest must be held for a minimum period of one year; (iii) the transferor must not be tax-transparent; (iv) the company whose shares are disposed of must either: (a) be liable to IRC in Portugal without benefiting from an exemption; (b) if resident in the EU, be liable to a tax referred to in Article 2 of Directive No. 2011/96/EU without benefiting from an exemption; or (c) if resident in a non-EU jurisdiction, be liable to a tax which is similar to the IRC, where the applicable rate is not below 60% of the Portuguese IRC rate (this condition may be waived under certain circumstances, which depend on the type of business of the subsidiary); (v) the entity whose shares are being disposed of should not be a resident of a country, territory or region included in the Portuguese blacklist; and (vi) no more than 50% of the value of the subsidiary's total assets is comprised of real estate located in Portugal, unless such properties are used in connection with an agricultural, industrial or commercial activity (other than a real estate buy and sell activity).

[367] Some double taxation treaties (*convenções para evitar a dupla tributação*) (DTT) entered into by Portugal also establish a waiver of taxation regarding capital gains obtained from the sale of a resident company, provided that such capital gains are not allocated to a PE located in the Portuguese territory.

[368] Additionally, a rollover relief mechanism may be used to exclude from taxable income 50% of the positive balance of capital gains and losses realised on the sale of tangible fixed assets, intangible assets and non-consumable biological assets, held for at least one year, to the extent that the realisation value of such assets is wholly or partially reinvested in the acquisition, production or construction of similar assets during a four-year period (i.e., one year before, the year of the realisation itself and the two years after the taxable period in which the realisation occurs). In case of a partial reinvestment, a partial relief (proportional to the investment made) will apply. When the reinvestment is not fully made until the end of the reinvestment period, the income that was not previously recognised for tax purposes must be subject to taxation in that period, increased by 15%.

4.2.2 Non-residents

[369] Non-resident taxpayers who do not have a Portuguese-situs PE may be subject to taxation on Portuguese-source capital gains realised on the disposal of the following assets: (i) Portuguese-situs real estate; (ii) the disposal of shares in real estate-rich companies (whether or not such companies are resident for tax purposes in our country); or (iii) the disposal of shares in Portuguese companies.

[370] There is an exemption that applies to non-resident entities or individuals deriving Portuguese-source capital gains from the disposal of shares and other securities issued by Portuguese entities, but this exemption does not apply in the following cases: (i) to non-resident entities domiciled in a blacklisted country, region or territory; (ii) to non-resident entities that are directly or indirectly held, as to more than 25%, by resident entities, except when cumulatively: (a) the non-resident entity is liable to a tax referred to in Article 2 of Directive No. 2011/96/EU without benefitting from an exemption or, if resident outside the EU, to a tax which is similar to IRC, where the applicable rate is not below 60% of the Portuguese IRC rate; (b) the non-resident disposing of the interest has held directly and/or indirectly at least 10% of the share capital or voting rights of the Portuguese entity issuer for a minimum period of one year prior to the disposal; and (c) the non-resident entity is not part of an artificial arrangement/arrangements, put in place with the main purpose or with the main purposes of obtaining a tax advantage; (iii) when more than 50% of the total assets of the Portuguese entity whose shares are being disposed consists of immovable property located in Portugal; and (iv) when the entity whose shares are disposed of actively manages or passively holds control in other Portuguese-resident companies, whose assets are made up as to more than 50% of immovable property located in Portugal.

4.2.3 Value Added Tax or Sales Taxes or Other Taxes on Revenue/Sales

[371] Supplies of goods and services are generally subject to Portuguese value added tax (*imposto sobre o valor acrescentado*) (VAT or IVA). Tax rates applicable on the Portuguese mainland are the standard rate of 23%, the intermediate rate of 13% and the reduced rate of 6%. In the Madeira Archipelago, the rates are 22%,

12% and 5%, respectively, while the tax rates applicable in the Azores Archipelago are 16%, 9% and 4%, respectively.

[372] There are few transactions excluded from VAT, the most notable being the transfer of a business as a going concern (*trespasse*), but there are a significant number of exemptions, e.g. financial and insurance services and real estate transactions (transfers and leases).

4.2.4 Stamp Duties or Other Taxes on Land Transactions

[373] Portuguese stamp duty may apply to acts, contracts, papers, documents, titles, and other facts occurring or deemed to occur within Portuguese territory as listed in the General Table of the Stamp Duty Code (*Tabela Geral do Código do Imposto de Selo*), which are not subject to or exempt from VAT. This territoriality rule is expanded under several rules, including the taxation of loans and guarantees granted by non-resident companies to Portuguese-resident entities, irrespective of where the contracts are materially executed.

[374] In this regard, it is worth noting that stamp duty applies, *inter alia*, to the following transactions: (i) the acquisition of immovable property (including by virtue of donation) at a rate of 0.8%; (ii) gifts and other gratuitous transfers to individuals; (iii) guarantees, including fees charged in connection therewith; (iv) the use of credit, in any form (including capital and interest), at rates that vary according to the maturity of the loan, as follows: (a) less than one year at a rate of 0.04% (per month or part of a month); (b) one or more years at a rate of 0.5%; (c) five or more years at a rate of 0.6%; and (d) credit in the form of a current account, bank overdraft or any other form in which the maturity is not determined or determinable at a rate of 0.04% on the average monthly balance; (v) interest charged by credit institutions, financial companies or other financial entities at a rate of 4%; (vi) sales as a going concern at a rate of 5%; (vii) repos (*acordos de recompra*); or (viii) the net asset value of collective investment vehicles.

[375] Some exemptions may be available, of which the most relevant are (i) on shareholder loans where the parties establish an initial period of not less than one year during which no early repayment occurs; (ii) an exemption for intra-group loans (despite being subject to several requirements related to maturity and distribution of the funds); and (iii) a general exemption for bond issuances.

[376] Portuguese property transfer tax or IMT is levied on the transfer of real estate located in Portuguese territory for consideration. IMT is due on the acquisition value agreed by the parties or the tax registration value of the immovable assets, whichever is higher. Tax rates applicable vary from 0.5% to 6.5%. This can be increased to 10% if the acquirer is domiciled in a backlisted jurisdiction or if the acquirer is an entity controlled by an entity domiciled in a backlisted jurisdiction.

[377] Owning real estate in Portugal – which entails the right to full and exclusive ownership of a real estate property (and this can also include usufruct or the surface right of immovable assets) – is generally subject to Portuguese real estate tax (*imposto municipal sobre os imóveis*) (IMI), which is levied annually at a rate ranging

from 0.3% to 0.45% (urban properties) of the tax registration value of the immovable assets located in Portugal; but the rate shoots up to 7.5% of that same value for properties owned by entities located in tax havens, or entities controlled by an entity domiciled in a backlisted jurisdiction. There is an Additional Tax to the IMI (*adicional ao IMI*) (AIMI), which aims to tax Portuguese real estate worth over EUR600 000.00 (the taxable basis corresponds to the sum of the tax registration value of all the properties held by each taxpayer, although there are some exceptions, such as urban properties classified as 'trade, industry, or services' and 'others'), regardless of where the owners are resident. Tax rates applicable are 0.4% for properties held by companies, 0.7% for individuals and 1% for those whose share in a Portuguese property exceeds EUR1 000 000.00. However, AIMI can be offset against personal income tax (imposto sobre o rendimento das pessoas singulars) (IRS or PIT) or IRC. The property tax value/tax registration value of real estate property may be subject to revaluation by the AT, which may result in an increase in the IMI and AIMI bill.

4.2.5 Business Rates

[378] Special levies/business rates may also apply to companies operating in specific industries, such as the energy and banking sectors, among others.

4.2.6 Taxes Imposed on Employers (e.g., *PAYE and Social Security Obligations*)

[379] The Portuguese social security system is financed by contributions from both employers and employees. Employers are required to pay up to 23.75% for employment contracts based on the actual salary. This contribution has no ceiling. The employer's social security contributions are deductible for IRC purposes.

4.2.7 Customs and Excise Duties

[380] Customs duties are regulated by the Community Customs Code. Therefore, the rules envisaged for the import and export of goods in Portugal are similar to the rules applicable in other EU Member States.

[381] Portuguese tax law provides different types of excise duties, such as petroleum and energy products tax, alcohol and alcoholic beverages tax, sugar-sweetened beverages tax, tobacco tax and vehicle tax, all of which are in line with related EU Directives.

4.2.8 Incentives by Way of Capital Allowances or Other Deductions in Respect of Capital Expenditure

[382] Portuguese tax law stipulates that resident companies are entitled to deduct 7% of share capital contributions not exceeding EUR2 000 000.00, which represent cash contributions of the shareholders, the conversion of shareholder loans, or

through the use of profits of the tax period itself, within the context of the incorporation of the company or the increase of its share capital, provided certain conditions are met. The deduction will be made in the tax period in which the entries are made, as well as in the following five tax years.

4.3 Tax Consolidation: Group Relief of Gains and Losses

4.3.1 Scope for the Use of Gains or Losses of the Target Company Elsewhere Within the Purchaser's Group

[383] Portuguese tax law does not provide a tax consolidation or fiscal unity regime but rather an optional tax regime under which the 'dominant company' (*sociedade dominante*) of a 'group of companies' (*grupo de sociedades*) may elect to aggregate the taxable profits and losses of any other company pertaining to the same group of companies ('Special Taxation Regime for Groups of Companies' – '*Regime Especial de Tributação de Grupos de Sociedades*', or RETGS).

[384] Under the RETGS, a group of companies exists when a company (the dominant company) directly or indirectly holds 75% of the share capital of another company or companies (the member companies) as long as such interest provides the dominant company with the majority of the voting rights in each of the member companies. An election to apply the RETGS can only be filed when certain conditions applicable to the dominant company and to the member companies are cumulatively fulfilled. Such requirements include, *inter alia*, that: (i) all the entities forming the group of companies have their headquarters or place of effective management in Portugal (under certain circumstances, it is possible for the dominant company to be a resident of an EU or EEA country or a Portuguese-situs PE of an EU or EEA resident company); (ii) all the entities forming the group of companies (including the dominant company) are subject to IRC, with all income being taxed at the highest general IRC rate applicable; (iii) the dominant company must have held a qualifying interest in a (the) member company(ies) for more than one year, on the date it intends to start applying the regime. The RETGS can apply with respect to newly incorporated member companies immediately, provided that the ownership/vote requirements are fulfilled as at the date of incorporation of such member company; (iv) the dominant company should not be controlled by another Portuguese company fulfilling the requirement to be the dominant company of a RETGS group; (v) the dominant company should not have opted out of the RETGS in the three years preceding the date on which it intends to start applying the regime; and (vi) the member companies cannot adopt a different tax period from the dominant company.

[385] The RETGS ceases to apply when any of the mandatory requirements concerning the dominant company are no longer fulfilled or when the taxable profits of any of the entities forming the group of companies (including the dominant company) are determined according to an indirect assessment. When a dominant company becomes controlled by another Portuguese company which fulfils the requirement to be considered a dominant company (other than the requirement with respect to losses during the three previous tax periods) during the application of the RETGS, the latter may elect to continue to apply the RETGS. Specific and strict rules apply to the carryforward of losses during the application of the RETGS, including in cases where a non-recognition transaction occurred. Also, pre- and post-RETGS loss carryforward is limited.

4.3.2 CFC Rules

[386] Portuguese tax law provides for controlled foreign company (CFC) rules, which closely follow the CFC regimes that have been adopted by several other EU Member States.

[387] The income generated by a CFC should be subject to taxation, irrespective of any dividend distribution, provided that certain requirements are met regarding the percentage of shareholding, the location of the foreign entity in a tax haven and the evaluation of profit generated by the relevant economic activity. As regards the shareholding percentages, the resident shareholders – whether individuals or companies – should hold at least 25% of the shares, voting rights, profit rights or assets of the relevant non-resident entity, directly, indirectly or by means of a fiduciary or an intermediary agent. With reference to the location criteria, a controlled company is an entity domiciled in a tax haven or an entity that is subject to an amount of tax on income that is less than 50% of the amount of tax that would be due in taxation under the rules set out in the Portuguese tax law. Finally, regarding the business activity requirement, CFC rules may not apply if the following types of income obtained by the relevant entity do not exceed 25% of its global aggregate amount of income: (i) royalties and other income from intellectual property rights, image rights and other similar rights; (ii) dividends and income arising from the sale of shares; (iii) income arising from financial leasing; (iv) income arising from banking business activities, even when not obtained by a credit institution, as well as from insurance activity or any other financial activities entered into with related entities; (v) income obtained by invoicing entities whose income arises from transactions with related entities; and (vi) interest and other capital income. These CFC rules do not apply when the foreign entity is resident in another EU or EEA jurisdiction (in the latter case, provided that the State in question is bound to administrative cooperation for tax purposes equivalent to the rules in force in the EU), and the resident shows that the establishment and activity of such foreign entity is grounded on valid economic reasons and that the entity carries out an agricultural, commercial or industrial activity, or renders services, using staff, equipment, assets and business facilities.

4.4 Tax Considerations Arising on M&A Transactions

4.4.1 Sale of Shares (For Cash, Shares or Other Securities)

From the Vendor's Perspective

[388] *Individual vendor:* Capital gains realised on the sale of shares by resident individuals are generally taxed at a WHT on account of the final tax payment at a 28% rate (Schedule 'G' income for PIT purposes) unless the individual chooses to include this income in his overall income and submit it to the progressive rate structure and the solidarity surcharge, or unless it is derived from shares of a non-listed micro or SME taxed at the effective rate of 14%. Notwithstanding the above, the balance between capital gains and capital losses on securities must be included in the taxpayer's overall income when they result from assets held for a period of less than 365 days and the taxpayer has a taxable income, including this balance, equal to or greater than the value of the last bracket of the general progressive IRS rates. Capital gains realised on the sale of shares of Portuguese tax resident companies, other securities issued by Portuguese tax resident companies, autonomous warrants issued by Portuguese tax resident companies, derivatives negotiated on the regulated stock markets or participation units in venture capital funds by non-resident individuals are generally exempt from PIT, unless these individuals are residents in tax havens or the shares disposed of are from companies whose assets consist, as to more than 50%, of real estate located in Portugal.

[389] The allocation, as a result of a share-for-share transaction, of the share capital of the acquired entity to the individual shareholders does not give rise to any taxation at the level of the shareholders if they carry-over the tax value of the old ones. *See also* answer below on 'rollover reliefs for share-for-share transactions' within the context of corporate reorganisations.

[390] For the calculation of capital gains or capital losses made in operations between an individual vendor and a related entity, the terms or conditions contracted, accepted and practised must be substantially identical to those that would normally be contracted, accepted and practised between independent/uncontrollable entities in comparable operations, applying the transfer pricing regime, with the necessary adaptations.

[391] *Corporate vendor*: Capital gains arising from the disposal of shares by resident corporate entities are not subject to taxation if, among other requirements, the shares disposed of have been held uninterruptedly for at least a twelve-month period, and the vendor holds directly or directly and indirectly, at least 10% of the share capital or of the voting rights.

[392] *See also* answer above on 'taxes on capital gains' and below on 'rollover reliefs for share-for-share transactions' within the context of corporate reorganisations.

From the Purchaser's Perspective

[393] *Individual and corporate purchasers:* Share deals generally do not give rise to VAT, stamp duty or real transfer estate tax at the level of the purchaser unless the deal in question involves Portuguese private limited liability companies (e.g., *sociedades por quotas or sociedades anónimas*) owning real estate and (i) the value of the company's assets derives, directly or indirectly, in more than 50% from immovable property situated in the national territory, considering the balance sheet value or, if higher, the VPT; (ii) such immovable property is not directly allocated to an agricultural, industrial or commercial activity, excluding the purchase and sale of real estate; and (iii) by that acquisition, amortisation or any other facts results in the acquirer owning, after the acquisition, at least 75% of the share capital of the company in question, or the number of individual partners is reduced to two (whether married or in a de facto union). In that event, the acquisition can be subject to Portuguese property transfer tax.

4.4.2 Sale of Assets (for Cash, Shares or Other Securities)

From the Vendor's Perspective

[394] *Individual and corporate vendors*: Excluding the transfer of a business as a going concern, forming an independent branch of activity (including the assets, liabilities and commercial relations of the vendor), the vendor, in principle, will charge VAT on the goods that are being sold, such as stock and movable assets, but each asset transferred will have its own VAT treatment (different tax rates). Immovable assets are exempt from VAT unless the exemption is waived by the vendor (which would allow the purchaser, where VATable, to deduct the input VAT), provided certain requirements are met.

From the Purchaser's Perspective

[395] *Individual and corporate purchasers*: If the transaction is not subject to VAT, an assessment must be made as to whether or not stamp duty should be levied. For stamp duty purposes, reference should be made to the transfer of a business as a going concern which is liable to stamp duty at a rate of 5% on its value. The purchaser must pay the stamp duty. The transfer of real estate is subject to property transfer tax and stamp tax, as previously explained.

[396] The transfer of real estate in the context of neutral reorganisations (e.g., mergers, spin-offs and contribution of businesses) may be exempt from property transfer tax, stamp duty and from all such emoluments and other legal charges as are due in restructuring processes.

4.4.3 Negotiability of the Price/Independent Assessment

[397] The value stipulated by the parties in an acquisition of immovable assets may be disregarded for tax purposes, as the applicable tax law states that this cannot be lower than the property tax registration value (i.e., the value previously appraised by the AT and registered for tax purposes). In general, the price and the conditions of any transaction where any related entities are involved must, in general, comply with the arm's length principle and, in particular, with the Portuguese transfer pricing regime, which is formed by the international transfer pricing framework enshrined in the OECD international instruments to which Portugal adheres and the specific Portuguese transfer pricing guidelines.

4.4.4 Tax Reliefs, Exemptions or Deferrals Available for Particular Types of Amalgamation or Reorganisation: Tax Clearances from the Relevant Tax Authorities

[398] As a result of the transposition of the EU Merger Directive, Portuguese domestic law provides for a special tax-neutral regime for certain operations performed as part of corporate reorganisations. Among other conditions, this regime provides a mechanism for the deferral of capital gains taxation on mergers, demergers, contributions in kind, share-for-share transactions, discounted securities (e.g., bonds) and transfers of tax residence performed for valid economic reasons (i.e., that do not have tax avoidance as their sole or main purpose). The Portuguese regime extends this regime to a broader set of transactions than those covered by the EU Merger Directive. The above-mentioned operations involve non-residents, but EU-resident companies may also benefit from the special tax-neutrality regime to the extent that they fulfil certain requirements.

[399] Domestic law also has a tax deferral mechanism in the exit tax payable upon the transfer of residence of Portuguese companies to other countries, which mechanism is in accordance with the case law of the European Court of Justice (ECJ) and provides for the option of: (i) immediate payment of IRC upon exit; (ii) an option for payment in five instalments; and (iii) an option for deferral until the year of effective disposal of the asset or transfer of residence to another EU/EEA country. In any case, taxpayers can request binding information from the tax authorities on the tax framework for certain transactions.

4.4.5 Unused Tax Losses in the Target Company/Restrictions on the Carry Forward of Losses

[400] As regards the carryforward of losses, this is available for resident entities for five years unless the entity is a certified SME, in which case the carryforward of losses is available for twelve years. For each year, the deduction of tax losses is capped at 70% of the taxable profit assessed in the tax year concerned. Carry-back is not allowed. Portuguese tax law establishes a general anti-loss trafficking rule that only deals specifically with direct acquisitions of shares, under which loss carryforwards are lost if more than 50% of the entity's ownership (share capital or voting rights) has changed between the taxable year in which such losses were generated and the end of the taxable year in which a deduction is claimed (i.e., a change of control of the target company). However, several exceptions apply to the general rule, such as (i) a change of ownership of the entity from direct to indirect and from indirect to direct; (ii) a change of ownership resulting from a tax-neutral reorganisation (mergers, divisions, partial divisions, transfer of assets and exchange of shares); (iii) a change of ownership arising from *mortis causa* succession; (iv) a change of ownership when the acquirer has held, directly or indirectly, more than 20% of the share capital or of the majority of the voting rights of the entity since the beginning of the taxable period to which the losses relate; or (v) where the acquirer is an employee or a board member, at least from the beginning of the tax period concerned.

[401] When no such exception applies, the Minister of Finance may approve the transfer of losses to the extent that a motion is filed with the AT and where it is considered that there is a recognised economic interest in authorising such transfer. In the case of non-resident entities, no carryforward of losses is available for business income unless such entities have a PE in Portugal.

[402] Non-residents that derive Portuguese-source capital gains and do not have a PE to which such gains are attributable are subject to tax on the balance of Portuguese-sourced capital gains and losses. In the case of securities, exemptions may apply.

4.4.6 Deferred Payments

[403] Where settlement of the consideration is deferred, the purchaser should address the following issues: (i) where the transaction involves related parties, interest may have to be charged over the deferral period to comply with the Portuguese transfer pricing rules; and (ii) where the deferral period is significant, there is a potential risk that the deferred consideration will be deemed as a financing/debt funding and for that reason subject to stamp duty.

4.4.7 Deductibility of Acquisition Expenses as a Business Expense

[404] In general, business expenses are deductible for tax purposes to the extent they are necessary to obtain or guarantee income subject to IRC. Formal requirements regarding the documentary support of such expenses should be observed. However, there are a few exceptions to the rule. For instance, the cost of acquisition of intangible assets (e.g., industrial property, such as patents, trademarks, permits, manufacturing processes, moulds or other similar rights acquired for a consideration or goodwill) from entities subject to a more favourable tax regime or from related parties, as defined for tax purposes, is disallowed as a tax-deductible expense.

4.5 Structuring the Investment

[405] Given the growing introduction of specific anti-abuse regimes within the EU context and also the onset of new duties on taxpayers to disclose possible tax avoidance schemes, any tax optimisation strategy, even if only general, should be preceded by proper tax advice by tax professionals.

4.6 Withholding Taxes

[406] As a general rule, dividends paid by Portuguese-resident companies to non-resident companies are subject to WHT at a 25% rate. This applies when the dividends are paid/made available to the shareholders. Furthermore, dividends, among other types of capital income, when paid or made available to accounts held by one or more holders on behalf of unidentified third parties or to entities deemed to be tax resident in blacklisted jurisdictions, suffer an aggravated WHT of 35%. Nonetheless, WHT on distributions of dividends may be exempt if eligible under a DTT, the Parent/Subsidiary Directive (PSD) or the domestic participation exemption regime.

[407] Dividends distributed by resident entities to non-resident entities are WHT exempt if the following requirements are met: (i) the beneficiary of the income is resident in another EU Member State, an EEA country that submits to administrative cooperation in a similar manner as between EU countries, or a country with which Portugal has executed a tax treaty that is in force and provides for the possibility of exchange of information; (ii) the beneficiary of the income holds, directly and/or indirectly, at least 10% of the share capital or voting rights of the distributing company; (iii) such participation has been held uninterruptedly during the twelve months prior to the distribution; and (iv) the beneficiary of the income is subject to and not exempt from any of the corporate income taxes referred to in the PSD, or is subject to and not exempt from a tax of a similar nature, with a statutory rate not lower than 60% of the Portuguese IRC rate. This regime also applies to dividends distributed by a resident company to PEs located in other EU or EEA countries of an entity that meets the above-mentioned requirements. It is also noteworthy that these exemptions are not applicable in case of abuse, in very similar terms to those foreseen in the PSD. This regime should also not apply if the Portuguese distributing company has not complied with the disclosure obligations prescribed by the Central Registration of Beneficial Owners Regime (*Registo Central do Beneficiário Efetivo*) (RCBE). Moreover, the Portuguese participation exemption also includes the anti-hybrid rule based on the Anti-Tax Avoidance Directive (Council Directive No. 2016/1164, 'ATAD 1'), pursuant to which it will not apply when the distributing company benefits from a deduction of the distributed outbound dividends.

4.6.1 Dividends Paid to Foreign Individual Shareholders

[408] Dividends paid to non-resident individuals are taxed at a final 28% WHT rate unless a reduction or elimination is provided for by the DTTs. Furthermore, dividends paid or made available to accounts held by one or more holders on behalf of unidentified third parties or to entities deemed to be tax resident in blacklisted jurisdictions are subject to WHT at the rate of 35%.

4.6.2 Dividends Received from Foreign Subsidiaries/Affiliates

[409] In principle, dividends received from foreign subsidiaries/affiliates are included in the taxable income of the Portuguese-resident corporate shareholder and thus subject to the general IRC rate. However, the participation exemption regime applies to dividends received from foreign subsidiaries/affiliates in the aforementioned conditions (*see* 'liability to tax' above). However, below that threshold, a Portuguese-resident shareholder may still be entitled to a full tax credit for the elimination of international economic double taxation.

4.6.3 Interest Paid to Foreign Corporate/Group Shareholders or Affiliates

[410] As a general rule, interest paid by Portuguese-resident companies to non-resident companies is subject to a 25% WHT rate upon maturity unless a reduction or elimination is provided for in DTTs, the EU Interest and Royalties Directive (IRD) or national law. Furthermore, interest paid or made available to accounts held by one or more holders on behalf of unidentified third parties or to entities deemed to be tax resident in blacklisted jurisdictions will be subject to WHT at the rate of 35%.

[411] Under the Portuguese rules that transpose the IRD, no WHT is due on payments of interest made by Portuguese-resident companies, provided that the following requirements are met: (i) the payer and the beneficial owner should be subject to and not exempt from IRC (or similar tax), and they must have one of the corporate types listed in the Annex to the IRD; (ii) both entities should be deemed to be EU-residents; and (iii) a direct 25% shareholding is required, or another company must directly hold at least 25% of the capital of both payer and beneficial owner, and in any scenario, the shareholding must be held for at least a two-year period.

[412] Interest on income paid by a resident financial institution or by a Portuguese branch of a foreign bank is exempt from WHT. Provided that the requirements set out in Decree-Law No. 193/2005 of 7 November are met, interest from debt securities (such as bonds) issued by Portuguese companies and made available to non-resident companies and/or individuals may also be exempt from WHT.

[413] Apart from WHT, interest payments may also trigger significant stamp duty charges, although some exemptions may apply.

4.6.4 Interest Received from Foreign Corporate/Group Shareholders or Affiliates

[414] In principle, interest received from foreign subsidiaries/affiliates is included in the taxable income of the Portuguese-resident corporate shareholder, thus, subject to the general IRC rate.

4.6.5 IP Royalties Paid to Foreign Corporate/Group Shareholders or Affiliates

[415] As a general rule, royalties paid by Portuguese-resident companies to non-resident companies are subject to WHT at 25% unless a reduction or elimination of tax is provided for in DTTs, the IRD or national law. Furthermore, royalties paid or made available to accounts held by one or more holders on behalf of unidentified third parties or to entities deemed to be tax resident in blacklisted jurisdictions suffer an aggravated rate of 35%. Moreover, payments made in connection with offshore IP may not be deductible if the Portuguese-resident paying company is not able to demonstrate that the payments relate to actual economic operations and that the price paid is not exorbitant.

[416] Under the internal rules that transpose the IRD, no WHT is due on payments of IP royalties made by Portuguese-resident companies, provided the following requirements are met: (i) the payer and the beneficial owner are subject to and not exempt from an income tax, and they match one of the corporate types listed in the Annex to the IRD; (ii) both entities should be EU-residents; and (iii) there is a direct 25% shareholding relationship between the two entities or another company holds at least 25% of their share capital, in both cases for at least two consecutive years.

4.6.6 IP Royalties Received from Foreign Corporate/Group Shareholders or Affiliates

[417] Royalty income is included in the IRC income as any other type of capital income. However, the Portuguese 'patent box' regime provides for a deduction corresponding to 85% of the income derived as consideration for the disposal or temporary use of certain industrial property rights (patents and industrial models) and copyright in computer programs, including income from the violation of such rights ('qualifying income'). Qualifying income is defined as the net positive balance between the revenues and gains derived in a given taxable year as consideration from the disposal or use of qualifying industrial property rights and the R&D expenses or losses incurred or borne in the same period by the taxpayer in connection with the industrial property right from which the gain is obtained. This regime does not apply to any services supplied which are ancillary to a qualifying disposal or temporary use of industrial property. As such, whenever included in an invoice for multiple services, royalties covered by this benefit must be segregated from the consideration for other types of services. This regime is subject to further conditions: (i) the transferee must use the industrial property in a business activity qualifying as an 'agricultural, industrial or commercial activity'; (ii) the licensing of the intangible must not generate a double dip (i.e., a double tax deduction) arising from triangular-type transactions between the licensor and related companies; (iii) the transferee cannot be a resident of a blacklisted jurisdiction; and (iv) the transferor must keep accounting records that identify the R&D expenses connected with the licensed intangible eligible for the patent box so as to enable the computation of the 'patent box' net income.

[418] Only that part of the 'patent box' income from an intangible that exceeds the accumulated negative balance between revenues and gains derived from that intangible in previous years will be deductible. The amount deductible amounts to 85% of the difference between the gross income from the licensing of covered intangibles and the lower of 130% of the quotient of the qualifying eligible R&D expenses or the total R&D expenses incurred (eligible R&D expenses exclude those that have been incurred by acquisition from related parties). Thus, computation of the 'patent box' income follows the OECD-*modified nexus approach*.

4.6.7 Management or Consultancy Fees Paid to Foreign Corporate/ Group Shareholders or Affiliates

[419] Management or consultancy fees (excluding those related to transportation, communication and financial activities) paid to foreign corporate/group shareholders or affiliates are, in general, subject to a WHT rate of 25%. However, tax treaties generally exempt these payments from WHT in Portugal.

[420] As a rule, and assuming that they are deemed necessary for the business of the local affiliate, payments regarding management and administrative expenditures made to non-local affiliates are deductible for tax purposes. Formal requirements regarding the documentary support of such expenses should be observed. The terms and conditions related to the rendering of those services and the payment of the relevant fees are subject to the transfer pricing rules and therefore should be made according to the arm's length principle. Otherwise, the AT may totally or partially deny the deductibility of such expenses for tax purposes. Moreover, payments made in connection with tax havens may not be deductible if the Portuguese-resident paying company is not able to demonstrate that the payments relate to actual economic operations and that the price paid is not exorbitant.

4.6.8 Payments to Non-residents in Respect of the Purchase or Renting of Immovable Property

[421] Capital gains on the sale of immovable assets and rents from urban, rural or mixed properties are classified as taxable income for IRC purposes and, when paid to non-residents, will be subject to a WHT rate of 25%. If the investor is a non-resident individual, consideration or rents will be treated as taxable income for PIT purposes and will be liable at a 28% flat rate, net of deductible expenses, namely *improvement* (computation of capital gains) and maintenance and repair, as well as the annual IMI paid (computation of rental income).

4.6.9 Double Tax Treaties Affecting the Payment of Withholding Taxes and the Main Requirements for Obtaining Relief from the Obligation to Withhold under these Treaties

[422] Portugal has so far signed eighty double tax treaties, seventy-eight of which are in force. As a member of the OECD, Portugal follows the OECD Model, a notable exception being the tax treaty with the USA, which follows the US Model.

Portugal also ratified and approved the Multilateral Convention to Implement Tax Treaty Related Measures to Prevent Base Erosion and Profit Shifting ('Multilateral Instrument' or 'MLI') and, being a member of the EU, benefits from all the EU legal instruments aimed at reducing double taxation within the Union.

[423] Beyond these bilateral and multilateral instruments, Portugal unilaterally grants unilateral tax credits for international, economic (dividends) and juridical double taxation. The method for elimination of juridical double taxation closely follows the OECD model, and economic double taxation is available for shareholdings of more than 10% and a minimum twelve-month holding period which are not eligible for the participation exemption.

4.7 Debt Financing

[424] In general, business expenses, including financing expenses (e.g., interest), are deductible for tax purposes to the extent they are necessary to obtain or guarantee income subject to IRC. Formal requirements regarding the documentary support of such expenses should be observed. There are, however, certain limitations that are applicable to the deductibility of interest expenses. For example, when the lender owns less than 20% of the borrower's share capital, interest payments from shareholder loans are not deductible on the excess of (i) the twelve-month Euribor rate plus a 2% spread, or (ii) the twelve-month Euribor rate plus a 6% spread, if the borrower is an SME. Above that shareholding percentage, the general transfer pricing rules apply. *See also* answer below on 'thin capitalisation' and 'transfer pricing'.

4.8 Thin Capitalisation

[425] The current quantitative IRC rule for limitation of interest deductions is no longer a traditional thin cap rule (where the deductibility of interest could be limited above a certain debt/equity ratio), but an EBITDA-based interest limitation rule which has been enacted before the advent of the ATAD 1, but which is fully in line with it.

[426] Net interest expenses may be deducted up to the greater of the following limits: (i) EUR1 000 000.00; or (ii) 30% of EBITDA as determined by accounting rules and corrected for tax purposes.

[427] It is possible to carry forward excess interest deductions and unutilised limits for five taxable years. Excess passive income is applied on a first-in, first-out basis after the current year's interest is deducted. The anti-loss trafficking rules detailed above also apply to excess interest deductions and unutilised limits. Tax groups within RETGS may elect to apply these rules on a group basis. However, the interest limitation does not apply to entities that are subject to the supervision of the

BdP or the ASF (Portuguese financial or insurance institutions), nor to the Portuguese branches of credit institutions and other financial institutions or insurance companies, or securitisation companies.

[428] Additionally, Portuguese transfer pricing rules may limit the deductibility of interest in the case of debt arrangements entered into with related parties, as defined for tax purposes, to the extent such interest is not established according to the arm's length principle.

4.9 Transfer Pricing

[429] As a general rule, Portugal follows the OECD standards on transfer pricing; the AT is thus legally entitled to challenge agreements established by *related parties* – roughly, those that have a direct or indirect 20% shareholding relationship or which may exercise a significant influence in the other's decisions – which contravene the arm's length principle. As of 2019, their scope encompasses not only commercial transactions but also corporate operations such as mergers, divisions and spin-offs.

[430] Determination of the arm's length price must be primarily carried out via the traditional transfer pricing methods (*comparable uncontrolled price, resale minus* and *cost-plus*), and only if they are deemed not to be adequate may the transactional methods come into play. Whenever in a transaction between two Portuguese entities, one of them suffers a primary transfer pricing adjustment, the AT has the duty to carry out a secondary adjustment to the taxable profits of the related counterpart, thus eliminating a possible double taxation.

[431] A way to mitigate the risks arising from transfer pricing adjustments is to enter into an Advanced Pricing Agreement (APA), whereby the transfer prices can be settled for a maximum of four years in an instrument binding on both the AT and the taxpayer (unilateral APA). The possibility of extending the APA to other tax authorities (multilateral APA) is also provided.

[432] Only in recent times has the AT begun to direct more of its resources towards transfer pricing inspections, but up until now, we have not seen a steep increase in litigation in the transfer pricing area. However, in its latest reports on combatting tax fraud and evasion, the AT highlights the increase in the use of international mechanisms available for the exchange of tax information as an important new pillar of tax audit activities. This may signal that we can expect a substantial increase in the control and audit of intra-group cross-border transactions and a possible surge in transfer pricing inspections.

[433] On 26 November 2021, Ministerial Order no. 267/2021 revised the rules on procedures for concluding APAs, and Ministerial Order no. 268/2021 introduced relevant changes to Portuguese regulations on transfer pricing matters by revising the formerly applicable Ministerial Order no. 1446-C/2001, which had been in force for twenty years. In general, the new legislative options reflect the international transfer pricing policy changes of the last few decades as per the revised

OECD Guidelines on transfer pricing matters, as well as the EU Joint Transfer Pricing Forum, aligning even more closely the Portuguese transfer pricing legal framework and the regulations in place in most of the OECD jurisdictions.

5 EMPLOYMENT CONSIDERATIONS

5.1 Legislative Framework

[434] In Portugal, the main legislative framework affecting employment matters is constituted by two general diplomas regarding Employment and Pensions: PLC, approved by Law No. 7/2009 of 12 February, and the Social Security Contributory Code (*Código dos Regimes Contributivos do Sistema Previdencial de Segurança Social*), approved by Law No. 110/2009 of 16 September, respectively. Moreover, there are several other legislative instruments regulating specific labour and social security issues, namely (i) the labour and social security misdemeanours procedural regime (*Regime processual aplicável às contra-ordenações laborais e de segurança social*), approved by Law No. 107/2009 of 14 September; (ii) the safety and health at work legal regime (*Regime jurídico da promoção da segurança e saúde no trabalho*), approved by Law No. 102/2009 of 10 September; (iii) the work accidents and occupational diseases regime (*Regime de reparação de acidentes de trabalho e de doenças profissionais*), approved by Law No. 98/2009 of 4 September; (iv) the age and invalidity retirement regime (*Regime de proteção nas eventualidades invalidez e velhice dos beneficiários do regime geral de segurança social*), approved by Decree-Law No. 187/2007 of 10 May; and (v) the unemployment protection regime (*Regime jurídico de proteção social da eventualidade de desemprego dos trabalhadores por conta de outrem*), approved by Decree-Law No. 220/2006 of 3 November, among others.

5.2 Employment Protection

[435] Portuguese Labour Laws provide employee protection rules, including in the case of business transfers.

[436] First, prior to the business transfer, information and consultation duties must be complied with, specifically:

(i) the vendor must inform the Portuguese Governmental Authority for Work Conditions (*Autoridade para as Condições do Trabalho*) (ACT) about the content of the contract between vendor and purchaser and also about all the elements which compose the relevant business unit;
(ii) the vendor and purchaser must inform workers' representatives and employees in writing about the date and reasons for the transfer, its legal, economic and social consequences and also the content of the contract between the vendor and purchaser. This information must be provided at least ten working days prior to the consultation of workers' representatives;

(iii) before the transfer, the vendor and purchaser must consult workers' representatives (or, in their absence, the representative commission designated for the relevant employees) in order to discuss, negotiate and agree on measures which will apply to the employees, as a result of the transfer. The ACT may participate in this consultation;
(iv) the vendor may immediately inform the employees covered by the transfer about the end of that consultation and, if such is the case, about the content of the agreement; and
(v) the transfer may only occur seven working days after the end of the deadline for the designation of a representative commission or after the aforementioned agreement or consultation.

[437] Portuguese labour law provides for a principle of continuity of all employees affected in the business or undertaking being transferred since their employment contracts are transferred to the purchaser. The purchaser is not entitled to select particular employees to the exclusion of others and is obliged to provide and maintain the employees' previous entitlements, seniority and rights (e.g., remuneration, professional category and social benefits). Without prejudice to that principle, employees may oppose the transfer of their employment contract when (i) the transfer may cause them harmful damages, namely due to the purchaser's lack of solvency or difficult financial situation, or even (ii) if the new labour policies do not seem trustworthy and sustainable. Should this be the case, employees must inform their intention to their employer in writing within five working days following the end of the deadline for the designation of the representative commission or after the agreement or the end of the consultation with workers' representatives. This opposition impairs the transfer of the employer's position, which remains with the vendor.

[438] Thus, in the context of business transfers, not only does the national regime provide extensive protection for affected employees, but it also equips workers' representatives with the rights of information and consultation prior to the transfer.

[439] Portuguese labour rules concerning the transfer of a business may only be derogated by collective bargaining agreements stipulating more favourable provisions for the employees.

[440] PLC also provides for information and consultation rights in the case of other corporate transactions, namely mass redundancies (collective dismissals and dismissals due to extinction of job position) and layoffs. Specifically:

(i) *Collective dismissal:*
(a) the procedure for collective dismissal begins with a written communication addressed to the Work Council (*Comissão de Trabalhadores*) or, if there is no such council, to the Company Union or Inter-Union representative structure existing in the company (*Comissão Sindical* ou *Comissão Intersindical*) or, in its absence, to the potentially affected employees, who will be invited to nominate a representative committee that will act as the

representative structure for this purpose and which, subsequently, will be entitled to receive the written communication referred to above;

(b) the written communication must contain (1) a description of the legal grounds for dismissal; (2) a roll of the company's personnel, organised by sectors of activity; (3) the criteria that will determine the selection of employees to be dismissed; (4) the number of employees to be dismissed and their professional categories; (5) the term during which the collective dismissal will take place; and (6) the criteria for any possible general compensation to be granted to the affected employees without prejudice to any specific compensation established by law or collective agreement.

(c) a copy of the communication and the attached documents must also be sent to ACT;

(d) within a five-day period following the initial communication, a phase of information and negotiation between the company and the employees' representatives must be initiated in order to try to reach an agreement on the scope and effects of the measures taken, as well as to decide on possible alternative measures that could reduce the number of dismissed employees, namely: suspension of work, reduction of work, professional reconversion and reclassification, and early retirement. In this regard, ACT participates in this negotiation phase, and either the employer or the representative structures may nominate an expert to assist them in this stage;

(e) after a minimum of fifteen days after the initial communication, or as soon as an agreement has been reached, the employer may send a written communication to each of the dismissed employees containing the dismissal decision, expressly indicating the reasons for and date of the dismissal, the amounts of the compensation and the labour credits, as well as the manner, timing and place of their payments;

(f) on the same date, the employer must send to ACT the minutes of the negotiation meetings, as well as a list containing the name of each employee, address, date of birth and of admission to the company, social security situation, profession, category and salary, as well as any individual measure applied and the date planned for its implementation. On the same date, a copy of such list is addressed to the employees' representatives; and

(g) lastly, the termination of the employment contract must be communicated with the following prior notice: (1) fifteen days for employees whose seniority is less than one year; (2) thirty days for employees whose seniority is between one year and less than five years; (3) sixty days for employees whose seniority is between five years and less than ten years; and (4) seventy-five days for employees whose seniority equals or exceeds ten years.

(ii) *Dismissal due to extinction of job position:*

(a) the intention to terminate the employment contract based on extinction of the job position must be communicated in writing to the employees' representatives (Work Council (*Comissão de Trabalhadores*)) or, if there is no such Council, to the Company Union (*Comissão Sindical*) or Inter-Union (*Comissão Inter-Sindical*) representative structure in the company, and also, to the relevant Trade Union if affected employees are shop stewards) and to each affected employee;

(b) together with the communication, the employer must indicate (1) the reasons for the elimination of the job position, including the relevant section, (2) an explanation of the need to dismiss and their professional categories, as well as (3) the criteria that will determine the selection of employees to be dismissed;

(c) the involved employees and the employees' representatives have a fifteen-day period counted from the date of the initial communication to oppose in writing the elimination of the relevant position, notably alleging lack of grounds or that the employer has failed to comply with the requirements described above and also to propose alternatives mitigating the effects of the dismissal;

(d) within five business days counted from the date of the initial communication, employees' representatives and employees may request ACT to issue a report (having seven days to do so) on whether the employer has complied with the relevant requirements;

(e) after five days counted from the end of the fifteen-day period referred to above or from receipt of the report referred to in the previous point above, the employer may communicate to the employees the decision to terminate their employment agreements based on the extinction of their labour positions;

(f) a copy of the decision must be sent to the employees' representatives and to ACT. The decision has to be made in writing and must include (1) the reasons for the elimination; (2) the confirmation of the existence of the relevant requirements; (3) proof that the criteria for determination of which positions to extinguish have been followed; (4) an indication of the amounts of compensation due and of all the labour credits, as well as the intended manner, timing and place of their payment; and (5) the date on which the employment agreement will terminate. It must also be said that the termination of the employment contract must be communicated, observing the period of prior notice required for collective dismissals.

(iii) *Layoff*:

(a) the procedure for layoffs begins with a written communication addressed to the Work Council or, if there is no such council, to the Company Union or Inter-Union representative structure existing in the company or, in its absence, to the potentially affected employees, who will be invited to nominate a representative committee to act as a representative structure for that purpose and which, subsequently, will be entitled to receive the written communication referred to above. Alongside the intention to reduce or suspend the carrying out of work, this communication must contain: (1) the economic, financial or technical grounds for the measure; (2) the company's personnel chart, organised by sectors of activity; (3) the criteria that will determine the selection of the employees to be covered by the measure; (4) the number of employees to be covered by the measure and their respective professional categories; (5) the period of time during which the measure will be applied; and (6) training actions the employees will be provided with during the reduction or suspension of work (if applicable);

(b) within five days following the communication referred to above, an information and negotiation stage takes place between the company and workers' representatives in order to obtain an agreement regarding the procedural modalities, scope and duration of the measures to be implemented (a minute of the negotiation meeting, mentioning any agreed and/or divergent positions, opinions, suggestions and proposals on each side must be drawn up);

(c) upon an agreement being concluded or, if no agreement is reached, at least five days after the delivery of the above information, the company communicates in writing to each employee the specific measures to be implemented, mentioning expressly the relevant grounds and the beginning and end dates;

(d) on the same date, the company sends to workers' representatives and to Social Security: (1) the minutes of the negotiation meeting, and (2) a map containing the name, address, date of birth and of admission to the company, the situation regarding Social Security, job, professional category and remuneration, individually applied measures and the dates of the beginning and end of the application of the measure, in reference to each employee.

[441] Upon termination of the contract, employees have the right to receive the amounts corresponding to any salaries and subsidies that are still owed, as well as any compensation that is due arising from the termination of the contract (e.g., collective dismissal and dismissal due to extinction of job position). In these cases, employees affected by collective dismissal and dismissal due to extinction of job position will be entitled to (i) a compensation corresponding to twelve days of base salary and seniority allowance per complete year of seniority; (ii) a credit of hours corresponding to two work days per week, during the notice period; and also to (iii) the possibility of terminating the contract during the notice period, subject to a minimum of three working days in advance, without prejudice to the compensation referred to above.

[442] Compensation criteria and amounts, as well as prior notices and deadlines, may only be derogated by collective bargaining agreements which are more favourable towards the employees.

[443] Moreover, employees have six months or sixty days, respectively, depending on whether it is a case of collective dismissal or of extinction of job position, counted from the date of termination of the employment contract, to file judicial proceedings whereby the lawfulness of the dismissal may be verified. In general terms, should the basis for the decision to dismiss be non-existent, or should the employer fail to comply with the procedural requirements (including payment of compensation and other existing labour credits), the termination is unlawful, and the employee is entitled (i) to the remuneration he would have received between the date of dismissal and the court's final decision; (ii) to be compensated for all relevant damages (moral and pecuniary damages); and (iii) to choose between reinstatement in the company or an indemnity to be determined by the court calculated on the basis of fifteen to forty-five days of base remuneration and seniority premium for each year of service or part of a year, subject to a minimum equal to three months' pay.

[444] National labour laws do not distinguish between 'blue collar workers' and 'white collar workers'. Moreover, according to the PCC, and in relation to limited liability companies by shares, during the period for which they are appointed, the directors (i) may not exercise, either in the company or in companies which are in a controlling or group relationship with that company, any temporary or permanent functions under an employment contract (whether of a subordinate or autonomous nature); (ii) nor can they enter into any contracts for the provision of services when the functions of administrator cease. Also, when a person performing any of these functions in a company (or in companies which are in a controlling or group relationship) is appointed as a director of that company, the employment contract related to such functions is suspended. By contrast, in private limited liability companies by *quotas*, the Code does not place any prohibition on the possibility of employees occupying one or more seats on the respective company boards.

[445] According to PLC, remuneration is composed of the base salary and other regular and periodical payments (due to, for example, overtime and night work), either in cash or in kind. Generally, remuneration is paid monthly at the end of the month to which the salary refers. It is also mandatory to pay for a thirteenth month, due on the annual leave date(s), and for a fourteenth month (as a Christmas allowance, which must be paid by 15 December each year). In 2022, the minimum monthly wage was EUR705. Furthermore, employees may receive other amounts, such as bonuses (based on individual performance or on the company's turnover and results) or participation in the company's profits, among others, which, as a general rule, do not have retributive nature.

[446] National labour laws also set out a number of rules regarding working conditions. Specifically, the employer has an obligation to permanently ensure employees' health and safety conditions at work. To comply with such duty, the employer must follow a set of general principles focused on the prevention of work accidents and occupational illnesses. In general terms, those obligations can be summarised into a global one involving mobilisation of the necessary means to ensure: (i) technical preventive measures; (ii) training, information and consultation of workers; and (iii) internal or external Health and Security (H&S, *segurança e saúde no trabalho*) services. The employer's duties include funding all the company's activity regarding H&S, such as the organisation and functioning of H&S services and other preventive measures, such as risk exposure assessments, tests and other actions on occupational risks and health monitoring. An insurance policy to cover the risk of accidents at work must be taken out by the employer for all employees.

[447] In Portugal, the negotiation of collective bargaining agreements with the local workforce is very common. This is demonstrated by the fact that there are provisions in the PLC under which collective bargaining agreements constitute a specific source of labour law that may, in some cases, derogate from the rules of the Code itself.

5.3 Pensions

[448] In Portugal, employees are mandatorily subject to a general social security regime, under which both employees and employers must pay their contributions. In this context, specific obligations are imposed on the employer, such as various communications and reports that have to be complied with at the beginning, end (termination) or suspension of the employment agreement, including appropriate reasons, as well as on any change to the agreed type of contract (permanent or fixed term, part-time).

[449] Social security contributions must be paid monthly and are incurred by both employer and employee. The general global contributory rate is 34.75% of the contribution base. The employer is responsible for 23.75%, and the employee for 11%. However, the employer must deduct the employee's contributions from his gross wage and deliver them to Social Security. The scope of social protection granted to dependent employees covers the events of sickness, parenting, unemployment, occupational illnesses, invalidity, old age and death.

[450] In general, the contribution base comprises all forms of remuneration, whether in money or in kind, due to an employee in exchange for work rendered, as established by the employment agreement, CBA, law, or custom and practice (e.g., base remuneration, seniority payments, holiday and Christmas allowances). Bonuses are also reflected in the contribution base if paid regularly every five years or less, and the employee is entitled to receive it in accordance with objective and general criteria. The law expressly excludes some benefits from the contribution base, such as values assigned to complement social security benefits, family benefits or reimbursement of medical expenses.

[451] As regards, specifically, old-age retirement, a pension is granted depending mainly on the age of the employee (the minimum retirement age in 2022 is sixty-six years and seven months) and fulfilment of the minimum insurance period (which is currently fifteen years of service, whether consecutively or interrupted, with registration of remuneration).

5.4 Retention of Key Management and Employees

[452] Pursuant to Portuguese Labour Law, employees are free to terminate the employment contract, provided a prior notice (between fifteen and sixteen days, depending on the type of contract and its duration) is given. Taking this into account, should a company wish to avoid the departure of a management team

and/or of key employees, it may need to consider measures such as the renegotiation of labour conditions, permanence and/or non-competition agreements in order to discourage such an eventuality.

[453] Under Portuguese law, any agreements between employers which (i) prohibit the admission of an employee who worked for them or (ii) which provide for the payment of an indemnity if a particular former employee is engaged by them are null and void.

[454] According to PLC, during the employment agreement, the employee must be loyal to the employer, namely by (i) not negotiating in his own name or on behalf of a third party in competition with the employer, (ii) nor disclosing information concerning the employer's organisation, methods of production or business. Upon the termination of the contract, non-competition obligations may only be applicable if employer and employee have agreed on it and in accordance with strict legal constraints. Non-compete agreements are only lawful if made in writing, if the activity of the employee is likely to cause harm to the employer and provided a compensation amount is paid to the former employee during the non-competition period. As a general rule, the maximum duration of this period is two years. However, if the employee was assigned to an activity which, by its fiduciary nature, constituted a special relationship with the company or to an activity that gave the employee access to particularly sensitive information relevant in terms of competition, the duration of the agreement may be increased to up to three years.

5.5 Treatment of Foreign Employees

[455] There are no specific rules regarding foreign managers or directors. Although, in respect of foreign employees, one may distinguish between (i) citizens of EU or EEA Member States, citizens of countries with which the EU has concluded agreements providing for the free movement of people, citizens of third countries who reside in Portugal as refugees or beneficiaries of temporary protection and family members of Portuguese citizens or of foreign workers in one of these situations; and (ii) other foreign employees who do not fit in any of these categories. Regarding this last class of employees, the employer must verify that the candidate holds a residence visa or permit specifically granted for carrying out a professional activity as an employee in Portugal. For the same purpose, the company must also provide the candidate with an employment contract or a promise of an employment contract. Unfortunately, the process to obtain the visa or permit tends to be complex and lengthy, requiring the collection of several items of data, and most of the necessary formalities have to be conducted prior to the foreign employee entering Portugal. Citizens of the EU or EEA member states exempted from the need to obtain a visa or permit prior to residing and working in Portugal, who nevertheless intend to stay for more than three months, must register with the competent authorities.

[456] Also, according to PLC, employment contracts with foreign employees (who do not fall into any of the first categories listed in the paragraph above) must be in written form and must contain, among other things, the following details: (i) work permit number; and (ii) name(s) and address(es) of pension beneficiary(ies) in the event of a fatal accident. Also, the execution and termination of the contract must be communicated to the ACT. Nevertheless, as a general principle, foreign employees working on work permits are granted equal rights and obligations as national employees.

[457] As a rule, the Portuguese Social Security regime is mandatory for all employees working in Portuguese territory, regardless of their nationality. Exceptions may occur in certain cases (e.g., posted employees) or resulting from International Social Security Conventions entered into between particular countries.

[458] Apart from personal income tax, employees, board members (when not exempt) and self-employed workers all have to pay social security contributions on their remuneration at the general rate of 11% (self-employed workers may have to pay up to 25.2%). In addition, employers must also contribute on the same taxable basis at a general rate of 23.75%.

5.5.1 Directors' Liability

[459] According to PCC, as a general rule, the liability of each director must be secured by a bond (*caução*) within thirty days of his appointment or election under penalty of immediate termination of duties. Furthermore, this bond must be maintained until the end of the calendar year following the year of the termination of the relevant term of office, irrespective of its cause.

[460] The bond must be in the amount fixed in the agreement, which cannot be less than:

(1) EUR250 000.00 for (a) companies with shares admitted to trading on a regulated market; and (b) companies which are not wholly owned by another company with a Supervisory Board and which exceeds, for two consecutive years, two of the following three thresholds:
   - total balance sheet value: EUR20 000 000.00;
   - net business volume: EUR40 000 000.00; and
   - average number of employees during the year: 250.

(2) EUR50 000.00 for all other companies. In this case, the director may be released from posting a bond by means of (a) a decision of the General Meeting or the Constituent Assembly appointing the Board of Directors or the Sole Director; or (b) by a provision by the articles of association when the appointment has been made.

[461] Additionally, the law exempts non-executive and unpaid directors from the necessity to provide a bond.

[462] If the liability of the director is secured by an insurance contract, it must be constituted in favour of the indemnity holders, and its costs may not be borne by the company except to the extent that the indemnity exceeds the minimum referred to above.

6 FUTURE DEVELOPMENTS

[463] Decree-Law No. 19/2019 of 28 January, as amended by Law No. 97/2019 of 4 September, established a regime for real estate investment and management companies (*sociedades de investimento e gestão imobiliária*) (SIGIs). SIGIs are intended to relate to the (much anticipated in Portugal) real estate investment trusts (REITs). Due to some particularities of the regime, SIGIs have not yet achieved great success in Portugal. That said, the first Portuguese SIGI, Olimpo Real Estate Portugal, SIGI, S.A. (Ores Portugal), the product of a joint venture between Bankinter and Sonae Sierra, was listed on Euronext Access Lisbon, on 24 June 2020, on which Morais Leitão acted as legal counsel. More recently, Morais Leitão acted again as legal counsel of Bankinter and Sonae Sierra to set out a new SIGI (Atrium Bire SIGI, S.A.), which acquired, in August 2022, 'Atrium Saldanha', one of the most emblematic buildings of the city of Lisbon.

[464] As previously stated, the implementation in Portugal of EU anti-money laundering directives and ultimate beneficial owner directives has had an impact on disclosure requirements and formalities. This has also affected the engagement of counsel, with additional know-your-client (KYC) obligations, and requires the disclosure of certain ownership/control-related information. Although approved in 2017 and implemented through regulations in 2018, the ultimate beneficial owner regime has been postponed several times, and it was only in January 2020 that the regime became mandatory for all companies. As a consequence, all corporate transactions which involve a change to the ultimate effective beneficiaries of the company must be reported and registered. Secrecy on share ownership no longer exists; however, we believe that these additional formalities will contribute to an increase in transparency and certainty and, consequently, greater credibility for the Portuguese market.

[465] The Portuguese Securities Code has recently been subject to significant revision by Law 99-A/2021. This has impacted several disciplines, such as public offerings, takeovers and governance matters. Notably, the concept of public company ('*sociedade aberta*') – which had no equivalent in foreign systems – and its regulatory implications have been eliminated. These have been positive updates to the PSC that are expected to simplify the law and update it in accordance with foreign innovative experiences and render the Portuguese market more attractive for issuers and investors.

[466] Recent legislation on loan funds has created a new financing alternative for Portuguese companies, which already exists in other European jurisdictions, by allowing collective investment undertakings such as mutual funds, real estate investment funds and pension funds to grant loans directly to companies.

[467] Arbitration in Portugal has gradually gained importance, and in several sectors, it is now generally regarded as the most effective means of alternative dispute resolution. Lisbon has been chosen as the arbitration seat in an increasing number of international arbitrations, especially for litigation involving Portuguese-speaking African countries.

[468] We also anticipate an increasing focus by the supervisory authorities on data privacy and the cybersecurity sector.

[469] Although at the end of 2019, the state of the Portuguese economy announced a busy M&A market, particularly in the real estate sector (tourism, hospitality sector, logistics, offices and housing), the renewable energy sector and the technology sector, the outbreak of the world pandemic COVID-19 made predictions a good deal harder. According to the annual report by the consultancy TTR, in 2020, the Portuguese market recorded 379 transactions, of which 182 had disclosed values of EUR18 000 000 000.00.

[470] Last year showed signs of recovery: according to the annual report by the consultancy TTR, in 2021, the Portuguese market recorded a total of 553 transactions and moved EUR19 200 000 000.00.[46] The number of transactions represents a 31% growth compared to 2020, as well as a 2% increase regarding the capital raised.

[471] However, 2022 did not follow such a trend: according to the quarterly report by the consultancy TTR, the market recorded, until the third quarter of 2022, a total of 328 transactions and moved EUR8 700 000 000.00.[47] The number of transactions represents a 22% decrease in the number of transactions compared to the same period in 2021, as well as a 46% drop regarding the capital raised.

[472] In 2021, the transaction highlighted by TTR was the sale by the Sonae Group of a 24.99% stake in Sonae MC to Camoens Investments, an entity indirectly held by funds managed by CVC Capital Partners, valued at EUR528 m; and in 2022, TTR highlighted the acquisition of Smart Studios by Round Hill Capital, valued at EUR200 m. Morais Leitão acted as legal counsel in both transactions.

[473] In 2022, according to the TTR, real estate has been the most active sector so far, registering 77 transactions, followed by the Internet, software & IT Services sector, with 41 transactions.

[474] In the private equity sector, in 2021, PE funds made 51 investments, with a 30% growth in the number of transactions compared to the same period in 2020, while Venture Capital funds made 113 investments, representing an 85% increase in the number of transactions, marking a recovery from a year severely affected by the pandemic. Up to the third quarter of 2022, PE funds have made only thirty investments, with a 9% decrease in the number of transactions compared to the same period in 2021, but registering a 4% increase in capital raised. Venture Capital funds made 62 investments, representing a 25% decrease in the number of transactions.

[46] Relatório anual sobre o mercado transacional português – 2021 (2021 Annual report on the Portuguese transactional market) available at https://blog.ttrecord.com/relatorio-anual-sobre-o-mercado-transacional-portugues-2021/.

[47] Relatório do terceiro trimestre sobre o mercado transacional português – 2022 (2022 Third quarter report on the Portuguese transactional market) available at https://blog.ttrecord.com/relatorio-do-terceiro-trimestre-sobre-o-mercado-transacional-portugues/.

[475] On a final note, the legislative and regulatory process in Portugal is always very broad and dynamic and requires permanent updating and a proper background. Given this, local legal advice is vitally important and essential for the preliminary assessment of any potential operation.

www.ingramcontent.com/pod-product-compliance
Lightning Source LLC
Chambersburg PA
CBHW071355230926
51846CB00002B/561
9789403534466